Owl &  Other issues...

A SELF HELP MANUAL

**Navigating Teenage Life:
Your Comprehensive Guide to
Overcoming Challenges and Thriving**

STEVEN BUCK

Grosvenor House
Publishing Limited

All rights reserved
Copyright © Steven Buck, 2024

The right of Steven Buck to be identified as the author of this
work has been asserted in accordance with Section 78
of the Copyright, Designs and Patents Act 1988

The book cover is copyright to Steven Buck

This book is published by
Grosvenor House Publishing Ltd
Link House
140 The Broadway, Tolworth, Surrey, KT6 7HT.
www.grosvenorhousepublishing.co.uk

This book is sold subject to the conditions that it shall not, by way of
trade or otherwise, be lent, resold, hired out or otherwise circulated
without the author's or publisher's prior consent in any form of
binding or cover other than that in which it is published and
without a similar condition including this condition being
imposed on the subsequent purchaser.

A CIP record for this book
is available from the British Library

ISBN 978-1-80381-842-9
eBook ISBN 978-1-80381-843-6

Dedicated to my children.

Contents

Introduction	ix
• Welcome to Owl Stretching and Other Issues...	ix
• The Importance of Self-Help for Teenagers	ix
• Embracing Change and Growth	x
Part I: Mental Health and Well-being	**1**
Chapter 1: Understanding Anxiety	3
• Symptoms and Triggers	3
• Coping Strategies	12
Chapter 2: Managing Stress	15
• Stressors in Teenage Life	15
• Stress-Reduction Techniques	23
Chapter 3: Battling Depression	34
• Signs of Depression	34
• Seeking Help and Support	43
Chapter 4: Navigating the Social Media Maze	56
• Benefits and Pitfalls of Social Media	56
• Establishing Healthy Online Boundaries	65

Part II: Interpersonal Relationships   75

Chapter 5: Confronting Bullying   77
- Types of Bullying   77
- Strategies to Address and Prevent Bullying   78

Chapter 6: Eating Disorders and Body Image   87
- Recognizing Eating Disorders   87
- Promoting a Healthy Body Image   94

Chapter 7: Peer Pressure and Its Impact   101
- Sources of Peer Pressure   101
- Resisting Negative Influences   102

Chapter 8: Mastering Money Management   109
- Budgeting and Saving Tips   109
- Financial Responsibility for Teens   110

Part III: Personal Development   117

Chapter 9: Cultivating Motivation and Ambition 119
- Strategies for Boosting Motivation   119
- Achieving Goals   120

Chapter 10: Navigating Substance Use   126
- Understanding Drug and Alcohol Issues   126
- Making Informed Choices   127

Chapter 11: Interacting with Law Enforcement	134
• Rights and Responsibilities	134
• Positive Encounters with Police	145
• Legal Resources for Teens	150
Chapter 12: Building Healthy Relationships	151
• Communication Skills	151
• Resolving Conflict	157
Chapter 13: Bridging the Generation Gap	162
• Effective Parent-Teen Communication	162
• Connecting with Parents	167
Part IV: Personal Growth	**169**
Chapter 14: Personal Growth/Developing Empathy	171
• The Power of Empathy	171
• Empathy in Action	176
Chapter 15: Fostering Creative Thinking	179
• Cultivating Creativity	179
• Innovative Ideas from Teens	184
Chapter 16: Decision Making and Problem Solving	188
• Making Informed Decisions	188
• Approaches to Problem Solving	193

Chapter 17: Embracing Self-Awareness 198
- The Journey to Self-Discovery 198
- Self-Awareness Tools 199

Chapter 18: Personal Hygiene 204
- The Importance of Hygiene 204
- What to Do When Things Go Wrong! 206

Basic skills 208
- Cooking 208
- Cleaning 213
- Living with others 218
- Choose life 220

Introduction

Welcome to "Owl Stretching and Other Issues... a self help manual". This guide is your roadmap through the exciting, tumultuous, and transformative years of adolescence. Whether you're a teenager seeking guidance, a parent hoping to understand your teen better, or anyone interested in helping young people succeed, this book is designed to be your trusted companion on this incredible journey.

The teenage years are a time of profound change. You are no longer a child, but not quite an adult. You may be dealing with a range of emotions, facing challenging situations, and trying to discover who you truly are. It's a period marked by growth, self-discovery, and the development of skills that will shape your future.

This manual sets out examples, some with follow up information and some that you will need to research on your own.

The Importance of Self-Help for Teenagers

In this guide, we emphasize the importance of self-help for teenagers. Why? Because self-help empowers you to take control of your own life, make informed decisions, and build the skills necessary to overcome obstacles. It's about taking charge of your personal growth and well-being, and it's a journey that can lead to greater self-confidence, resilience, and happiness.

While adults, mentors, and teachers can offer valuable guidance, ultimately, it's you who must navigate the ups and downs of your teenage years. Self-help doesn't mean you're alone in this journey; it means you are actively involved in shaping your future. You have the power to make choices that reflect your values, aspirations, and dreams.

Embracing Change and Growth

Change is a constant companion during adolescence. Your body is changing, your mind is evolving, and your social landscape is shifting. Embracing these changes is essential to your well-being. We'll explore topics like anxiety, stress, and depression, which can be common companions on this journey, and provide you with strategies to manage them effectively.

As we delve into each chapter, you'll discover insights and tools that can help you overcome obstacles related to mental health, relationships, personal development, and more.

So, are you ready to embark on this journey of self-discovery and empowerment? Let's begin by exploring the challenges and triumphs that lie ahead, and let this guide be your trusted companion as you navigate the path of teenage life.

PART I

MENTAL HEALTH AND WELL-BEING

Chapter 1: Understanding Anxiety

In this chapter, we will explore the complex world of anxiety, a common and often misunderstood mental health condition that affects many teenagers. By delving into the symptoms and triggers, understanding the nature of anxiety, and learning effective coping strategies, you can take the first steps toward managing this challenging aspect of your teenage journey.

Symptoms and Triggers

Understanding Anxiety

Anxiety is a natural response to stress, but for some teenagers, it can become overwhelming and interfere with their daily lives. To effectively address anxiety, it's crucial to first recognize its symptoms and understand what might be triggering it. In this section, we will cover:

- Common Symptoms: Explore the physical, emotional, and cognitive symptoms of anxiety. Learn how to recognize when anxiety is at play in your life.
- Triggers: Identify the various factors that can trigger anxiety in teenagers. From academic pressures to social situations, understanding your triggers is the first step toward managing anxiety.

Understanding Teenagers and Anxiety: Symptoms, Triggers, and Management

Introduction

Teenage years are a period of rapid growth and development, marked by significant physical, emotional, and cognitive changes. It is during this phase that many adolescents grapple with the challenges of anxiety. Anxiety disorders are among the most common mental health issues affecting teenagers today, and they can manifest in various ways. To address this important issue, it is crucial to delve into the common symptoms of anxiety and explore the triggers that can lead to its onset in teenagers. By understanding these aspects, parents, educators, and teenagers themselves can better recognize and manage anxiety for improved mental well-being.

I. Common Symptoms of Anxiety in Teenagers

Anxiety is a natural response to stress or danger and can be a healthy, adaptive mechanism. However, when it becomes chronic and excessive, it can significantly impact a teenager's daily life. Understanding the common symptoms of anxiety is essential for early recognition and intervention. Anxiety symptoms can be categorized into three main areas: physical, emotional, and cognitive.

A. Physical Symptoms

   1. Increased Heart Rate: One of the most noticeable physical symptoms of anxiety is a racing heart. Teenagers experiencing anxiety may feel as if their heart is pounding or racing even when there is no apparent physical cause.
   2. Muscle Tension: Anxiety often leads to muscle tension, which can result in headaches, neck and shoulder pain, and even stomach-aches. This tension can be a manifestation of the body's "fight or flight" response.
   3. Sweating and Trembling: Sweating excessively or trembling, especially in stressful situations, is a common physical symptom of anxiety. This can be particularly distressing for teenagers when it occurs in public settings.
   4. Shortness of Breath: Anxiety can lead to rapid, shallow breathing or even hyperventilation, causing feelings of breathlessness and a sense of impending doom.
   5. Gastrointestinal Distress: Nausea, diarrhoea, and other gastrointestinal problems can arise due to anxiety. These symptoms can further exacerbate anxiety and create a vicious cycle.

B. Emotional Symptoms

   1. Excessive Worry: Teenagers with anxiety often experience excessive and uncontrollable worry

about a wide range of concerns, from academic performance to social interactions.

2. Irritability: Anxiety can make teenagers irritable and easily frustrated. They may become more prone to mood swings and outbursts of anger.
3. Restlessness: Restlessness is a common emotional symptom of anxiety. Teenagers may find it challenging to relax and constantly feel the need to be on the move or engage in distracting activities.
4. Fear and Avoidance: Anxiety can lead to specific fears or phobias, causing teenagers to avoid situations or places that trigger their anxiety. This avoidance can further limit their social and academic experiences.
5. Low Self-Esteem: Adolescents with anxiety may have negative thoughts about themselves, doubting their abilities and feeling inferior to their peers.

C. Cognitive Symptoms

1. Excessive Thinking: Teenagers with anxiety often engage in repetitive and distressing thoughts. These thoughts can be self-critical, catastrophic, or obsessive in nature.
2. Difficulty Concentrating: Anxiety can impair a teenager's ability to concentrate and focus on tasks, making it challenging to perform well in school or extracurricular activities.

3. Memory Problems: Anxiety may lead to forgetfulness and difficulty retaining information, which can further contribute to academic difficulties.
4. Cognitive Distortions: Anxiety often involves cognitive distortions, where teenagers interpret situations in a biased and negative manner. This can lead to unrealistic fears and anxieties.

Recognizing when anxiety is at play in a teenager's life involves identifying these symptoms and observing their frequency and severity. Early intervention can be crucial in preventing anxiety from escalating into a more debilitating condition.

II. Triggers of Anxiety in Teenagers

Understanding the triggers of anxiety in teenagers is essential for effective management. Several factors can contribute to the onset or exacerbation of anxiety in this age group.

A. Academic Pressures

1. High Expectations: The pressure to excel academically, whether self-imposed or coming from parents and educators, can create intense anxiety in teenagers. They may fear disappointing others or believe that their worth is solely determined by their grades.

2. Test and Exam Anxiety: The anticipation of tests, exams, and standardized assessments can trigger anxiety. Fear of failure or the consequences of poor performance can be overwhelming.
3. Time Management: Balancing a heavy workload, extracurricular activities, and social life can be challenging. Poor time management and the fear of falling behind can lead to anxiety.

B. Social Situations

1. Peer Pressure: Adolescents often face peer pressure to conform, which can lead to anxiety about fitting in and avoiding rejection.
2. Social Anxiety: Some teenagers experience social anxiety disorder, characterized by an intense fear of social situations and interaction with peers. This can make school and social events extremely distressing.
3. Bullying and Cyberbullying: Being a victim of bullying or cyberbullying can have long-lasting psychological effects, contributing to anxiety and feelings of insecurity.

C. Family Dynamics

1. Parental Expectations: High parental expectations, a demanding or critical parenting style, or the stress of family conflict can all contribute to a teenager's anxiety.

2. Divorce or Family Changes: Major family changes, such as divorce, relocation, or the addition of new family members, can disrupt a teenager's sense of stability and security, triggering anxiety.

D. Health and Lifestyle Factors

1. Substance Abuse: Experimentation with drugs or alcohol can lead to anxiety, both as a result of the substances themselves and the consequences of their use.
2. Sleep Deprivation: Irregular sleep patterns and insufficient sleep can negatively impact a teenager's mood and overall mental health, making them more susceptible to anxiety.

E. Traumatic Events

Trauma: Exposure to traumatic events, such as accidents, violence, or natural disasters, can lead to post-traumatic stress disorder (PTSD) and acute anxiety in teenagers.

F. Hormonal Changes

Puberty: The hormonal changes associated with puberty can exacerbate anxiety symptoms. Fluctuations in hormones can affect mood regulation and emotional well-being.

G. Genetic Predisposition

Family History: A family history of anxiety disorders can increase a teenager's risk of developing anxiety themselves, suggesting a genetic predisposition.

Recognizing the specific triggers that contribute to a teenager's anxiety is crucial for implementing targeted strategies and support systems to manage and alleviate these stressors.

III. Managing Teenage Anxiety

Once the symptoms and triggers of anxiety in teenagers are understood, it is essential to explore effective strategies for managing this mental health challenge.

A. Communication: Encouraging open and non-judgmental communication between teenagers and trusted adults, such as parents, teachers, or counsellors, can create a supportive environment for discussing anxieties and seeking help.

B. Psychoeducation: Providing teenagers with information about anxiety, its symptoms, and its prevalence can help reduce the stigma associated with mental health issues and empower them to seek assistance.

C. Cognitive Behavioural Therapy (CBT): CBT is a widely recognized therapeutic approach for treating anxiety. It helps teenagers identify and challenge negative thought patterns and develop coping strategies.

D. Medication: In some cases, medication prescribed by a qualified healthcare professional may be necessary to manage severe anxiety symptoms. Medication should always be used in conjunction with therapy and under medical supervision.

E. Lifestyle Modifications: Encouraging a healthy lifestyle with regular exercise, a balanced diet, and adequate sleep can have a significant impact on anxiety management.

F. Mindfulness and Relaxation Techniques: Practices such as mindfulness meditation and deep breathing exercises can help teenagers manage stress and anxiety by promoting relaxation and self-awareness.

G. Social Support: Building a strong support system through friendships and connections with peers can provide teenagers with emotional support and a sense of belonging.

H. Time Management and Stress Reduction: Teaching teenagers time management skills and stress reduction techniques can help them better cope with academic and social pressures.

I. Professional Help: In cases of severe or persistent anxiety, it is crucial to seek the assistance of mental health professionals, such as psychologists, psychiatrists, or counsellors, who can provide specialized treatment and support.

Teenage anxiety is a prevalent and often misunderstood issue that can significantly impact a teenager's well-being and development. Recognizing the common symptoms and triggers of anxiety is the first step in addressing this challenge effectively. By providing teenagers with the tools to manage their anxiety and offering a supportive environment, we can help them navigate the tumultuous teenage years with greater resilience and mental health. It is essential to remember that anxiety is a treatable condition, and with the right resources and support, teenagers can thrive and grow into confident and resilient adults.

Coping Strategies

Managing Anxiety

Once you've identified the symptoms and triggers of anxiety, it's time to explore practical coping strategies that can help you regain control over your thoughts and feelings. We'll delve into:

- Breathing Techniques: Discover the power of deep breathing exercises to calm your mind and reduce anxiety.

Take a deep breath in. Now let it out. You may notice a difference in how you feel already. Your breath is a powerful tool to ease stress and make you feel less anxious.

Some simple breathing exercises can make a big difference if you make them part of your regular routine.

Before you get started, keep these tips in mind:

Choose a place to do your breathing exercise. It could be in your bed, on your living room floor, or in a comfortable chair.

Don't force it. This can make you feel more stressed.

Try to do it at the same time once or twice a day.

Wear comfortable clothes.

Many breathing exercises take only a few minutes. When you have more time, you can do them for 10 minutes or more to get even greater benefits.

- Mindfulness and Meditation: Learn how mindfulness and meditation can help you stay present, reduce stress, and manage anxiety effectively.
- Cognitive-Behavioural Techniques: Explore cognitive-behavioural strategies to challenge and reframe anxious thoughts.
- Physical Activity: Understand the positive impact of regular exercise on anxiety levels and mental well-being.

Understanding anxiety is the first step toward managing it effectively. As we explore these symptoms, triggers, coping strategies, and real-life case studies, you'll gain valuable insights into this common mental health condition. Remember, you're not alone on this journey, and there are resources and strategies available to help you conquer anxiety and thrive during your teenage years.

Chapter 2: Managing Stress

Stress is an unavoidable part of life, and during your teenage years, you may encounter various stressors that can feel overwhelming. However, understanding how to manage stress effectively is a crucial skill that can help you navigate the ups and downs of adolescence. In this chapter, we will explore the stressors commonly faced by teenagers, effective stress-reduction techniques, and stories of success that demonstrate how individuals have triumphed over stress.

Stressors in Teenage Life

Recognizing the Challenges

Teenagers today face a multitude of stressors, some of which are unique to this stage of life. It's essential to recognize and understand these stressors to address them effectively. We will discuss:

- Academic Pressure: Explore the stress associated with exams, assignments, and expectations for academic achievement.
- Social Pressures: Examine the challenges of fitting in, forming friendships, and dealing with peer pressure.

- Family Dynamics: Understand the impact of family relationships and responsibilities on teenage stress levels.
- Extracurricular Demands: Discuss the stressors related to extracurricular activities, such as sports, clubs, and hobbies.
- Technology and Social Media: Analyze how digital life, including social media, can contribute to stress.
- Future Uncertainty: Address the anxiety that often accompanies questions about the future, such as career choices and college plans.

Empowering Teenagers: Strategies for Managing Anxiety

Introduction

Teenagers today face a multitude of challenges that can often lead to increased stress and anxiety. Academic pressures, social interactions, and the rapid physical and emotional changes that accompany adolescence can all contribute to feelings of unease. Fortunately, there are various effective strategies that teenagers can employ to manage and alleviate anxiety. This comprehensive guide explores four key techniques that can empower teenagers to take control of their mental well-being: Breathing Techniques, Mindfulness and Meditation, Cognitive-Behavioral Techniques, and Physical Activity. By incorporating these practices into their daily lives, teenagers can develop valuable skills to reduce anxiety, enhance resilience, and foster a positive outlook.

I. Breathing Techniques

Breathing is a fundamental and often overlooked aspect of managing anxiety. Deep breathing exercises can have a profound impact on calming the mind and reducing anxiety levels. Teenagers can benefit greatly from incorporating these techniques into their daily routines.

A. The Power of Deep Breathing

   1. Understanding the Autonomic Nervous System: Breathing techniques work by influencing the autonomic nervous system, specifically the sympathetic (fight-or-flight) and parasympathetic (rest-and-digest) branches. Deep, controlled breathing activates the parasympathetic nervous system, which promotes relaxation and reduces stress.
   2. Physiological Changes: Deep breathing leads to several physiological changes that counteract the stress response. These changes include a decrease in heart rate, lowered blood pressure, and reduced muscle tension.

B. Practical Deep Breathing Exercises

   1. Diaphragmatic Breathing: This technique involves taking slow, deep breaths, focusing on expanding the diaphragm rather than shallow chest breathing. To practice, teenagers can lie on their backs,

place a hand on their chest and the other on their abdomen, and breathe deeply, making sure the hand on the abdomen rises with each breath.
2. 4-7-8 Technique: Inhaling for a count of four, holding the breath for seven, and exhaling for eight can be an effective way to slow down the breath and induce relaxation.
3. Box Breathing: Box breathing involves inhaling, holding the breath, exhaling, and holding the breath again, each for an equal count (e.g., four seconds). This technique can be done discreetly in any situation.

II. Mindfulness and Meditation

Mindfulness and meditation are powerful tools for managing anxiety and promoting mental well-being. These practices encourage teenagers to stay present, reduce stress, and develop a deeper understanding of their thoughts and emotions.

A. The Essence of Mindfulness
   1. Being Present: Mindfulness involves paying deliberate attention to the present moment without judgment. It encourages teenagers to observe their thoughts, emotions, and sensations without getting caught up in them.

2. Reducing Stress: By focusing on the here and now, mindfulness can break the cycle of rumination and worry, reducing anxiety and promoting relaxation.

B. Practicing Mindfulness and Meditation

1. Mindfulness Meditation: Teenagers can start with short mindfulness meditation sessions. They sit in a comfortable position, close their eyes, and focus on their breath or a specific object or sound. When their mind inevitably wanders, they gently bring their attention back to the chosen point of focus.
2. Body Scan: This mindfulness exercise involves paying close attention to each part of the body, starting from the toes and moving up to the head. It helps release physical tension and can be particularly useful for reducing anxiety.
3. Mindful Walking: Encourage teenagers to take mindful walks, paying attention to the sensation of each step and their surroundings. This can be a refreshing way to connect with the present moment.
4. Guided Meditation: Many apps and online resources offer guided meditation sessions specifically designed for teenagers. These can be an excellent way to introduce mindfulness and meditation practices.

III. Cognitive-Behavioural Techniques

Cognitive-behavioural techniques are valuable tools for challenging and reframing anxious thoughts. These strategies empower teenagers to take control of their mental processes and change negative thinking patterns.

A. Understanding Cognitive-Behavioural Techniques

    1. Identifying Anxious Thoughts: The first step in CBT is recognizing anxious thoughts and patterns. Teenagers learn to distinguish between rational and irrational thoughts.
    2. Challenging Negative Beliefs: Once identified, teenagers can challenge negative beliefs by questioning their validity and considering alternative, more balanced perspectives.
    3. Restructuring Thoughts: CBT helps teenagers restructure their thoughts by replacing irrational or catastrophic thinking with more realistic and positive thoughts.

B. Practical Cognitive-Behavioural Techniques

    1. Journaling: Keeping a thought journal can help teenagers identify and track their anxious thoughts. They can then work on challenging and reframing these thoughts.
    2. The ABCDE Model: This model involves identifying the Activating event, Beliefs about the event,

Consequences of those beliefs, Disputing irrational beliefs, and Effect of the new belief. It's a structured way to address and reframe anxious thoughts.

3. Positive Self-Talk: Encourage teenagers to replace self-critical thoughts with positive affirmations. For example, they can replace "I'll never do well on this test" with "I'll do my best and learn from the experience."
4. Visualization: Visualization techniques involve imagining a successful outcome in a stressful situation, helping to reduce anxiety and boost confidence.

IV. Physical Activity

Regular exercise is a powerful tool for managing anxiety and improving overall mental well-being. Engaging in physical activity releases endorphins, reduces stress hormones, and fosters a sense of accomplishment.

A. The Benefits of Physical Activity

1. Endorphin Release: Exercise triggers the release of endorphins, which are natural mood lifters. This can have a positive impact on reducing anxiety and boosting mood.
2. Stress Reduction: Physical activity serves as a healthy outlet for stress and pent-up energy.

It helps alleviate tension and can improve sleep quality.
3. Enhanced Self-Esteem: Achieving fitness goals and feeling physically strong can boost self-esteem and confidence, reducing anxiety related to self-worth.

B. Incorporating Physical Activity into Daily Life

1. Find Enjoyable Activities: Encourage teenagers to choose physical activities they enjoy, whether it's playing a sport, dancing, hiking, or simply going for a brisk walk.
2. Establish a Routine: Creating a regular exercise routine can provide structure and consistency, which can help manage anxiety.
3. Social Engagement: Participating in team sports or group fitness classes can foster social connections, reducing feelings of isolation and anxiety.
4. Mind-Body Activities: Activities like yoga and tai chi combine physical movement with mindfulness, offering a dual benefit for anxiety management.

Teenagers face unique challenges in their lives that can lead to increased stress and anxiety. However, by incorporating the four key strategies discussed in this guide - Breathing Techniques, Mindfulness and Meditation, Cognitive-Behavioral Techniques, and Physical Activity -

they can empower themselves to take control of their mental well-being.

These practices are not standalone solutions; rather, they work synergistically to provide a holistic approach to anxiety management. Encouraging teenagers to explore and integrate these techniques into their daily lives can have a profound and lasting impact on their emotional resilience, stress reduction, and overall mental health.

It is important to emphasize that seeking professional help, when necessary, is a crucial part of managing anxiety. If a teenager's anxiety becomes overwhelming or persistent, a mental health professional can provide expert guidance and support. By combining these self-help techniques with professional assistance when needed, teenagers can navigate the challenges of adolescence with greater confidence and well-being

Stress-Reduction Techniques

Strategies for Coping

In this section, we will explore various stress-reduction techniques that can empower you to manage stress effectively. These techniques include:

- Mindfulness and Meditation: Learn how mindfulness practices can help you stay present, reduce anxiety, and manage stress.

- Time Management: Discover strategies for effectively managing your time and reducing the pressure of deadlines.
- Healthy Lifestyle Choices: Explore the connection between physical health and stress reduction, including the importance of nutrition, exercise, and sleep.
- Emotional Expression: Understand the significance of expressing your feelings and seeking support from friends, family, or professionals.
- Relaxation Techniques: Explore relaxation exercises, such as progressive muscle relaxation and guided imagery, to calm your mind and body.
- Coping Skills: Learn specific coping strategies to deal with stress in the moment, such as deep breathing and positive self-talk.

Empowering Teenagers: Strategies for Managing Stress and Promoting Well-being

Teenagers today face a multitude of challenges that can lead to stress and anxiety. Academic pressures, social interactions, physical and emotional changes, and the ever-present digital world can all contribute to feelings of overwhelm. However, it's crucial for teenagers to develop effective stress management strategies to cope with these challenges and promote their overall well-being. This comprehensive guide explores six key techniques that empower teenagers to take control of their lives:

Mindfulness and Meditation, Time Management, Healthy Lifestyle Choices, Emotional Expression, Relaxation Techniques, and Coping Skills. By incorporating these practices into their daily routines, teenagers can learn to manage stress, enhance their resilience, and foster a positive and balanced life.

I. Mindfulness and Meditation

Mindfulness and meditation are powerful practices that can help teenagers stay present, reduce anxiety, and manage stress effectively. These techniques encourage individuals to focus on the here and now, fostering a greater sense of inner calm and mental clarity.

A. The Essence of Mindfulness
   1. Present Moment Awareness: Mindfulness involves paying deliberate attention to the present moment without judgment. It encourages teenagers to observe their thoughts, emotions, and sensations without getting caught up in them.
   2. Reducing Stress: By focusing on the here and now, mindfulness can break the cycle of rumination and worry, reducing anxiety and promoting relaxation.

B. Practical Mindfulness and Meditation Exercises
   1. Breathing Meditation: This involves sitting comfortably and focusing on the breath. When the

mind wanders (as it inevitably will), gently guide your attention back to your breath. This practice enhances concentration and promotes relaxation.
2. Body Scan Meditation: This practice involves mentally scanning your body, paying attention to any areas of tension or discomfort and releasing them. It can be particularly effective for reducing physical stress.
3. Mindful Walking: Walking mindfully means paying close attention to each step and the sensations in your body as you walk. It's an excellent way to integrate mindfulness into everyday activities.
4. Guided Meditation: Many apps and online resources offer guided meditation sessions specifically designed for teenagers. These can be an excellent way to introduce mindfulness and meditation practices.

II. Time Management

Effective time management is a crucial skill for teenagers to reduce stress and manage the pressures of academics, extracurricular activities, and social commitments. By learning how to manage their time effectively, teenagers can reduce the pressure of deadlines and create a more balanced life.

A. The Importance of Time Management
1. Reduced Procrastination: Effective time management helps teenagers avoid procrastination and stay on top of their responsibilities.

2. Enhanced Productivity: Learning to prioritize tasks and allocate time wisely can significantly enhance productivity.
3. Stress Reduction: Properly managing time reduces the last-minute rush to meet deadlines, thereby reducing stress levels.

B. Strategies for Effective Time Management
1. Set Clear Goals: Define clear, achievable goals for both short-term and long-term tasks.
2. Prioritize Tasks: Identify the most important and urgent tasks and tackle them first.
3. Use Time Management Tools: Utilize tools like planners, digital calendars, or time management apps to schedule activities and stay organized.
4. Break Tasks into Smaller Steps: Divide larger tasks into smaller, manageable steps to make them less overwhelming.
5. Avoid Multitasking: Focus on one task at a time to improve efficiency and reduce stress.
6. Learn to Say No: Avoid overcommitting by politely declining additional responsibilities when necessary.

III. Healthy Lifestyle Choices

Teenagers often underestimate the connection between physical health and stress reduction. By making healthy lifestyle choices related to nutrition, exercise, and sleep, they can improve their physical and mental well-being.

A. The Connection Between Lifestyle and Stress

1. Nutrition: A balanced diet with plenty of fruits, vegetables, lean proteins, and whole grains provides the body with essential nutrients to manage stress.
2. Exercise: Regular physical activity releases endorphins, reduces stress hormones, and provides an effective outlet for stress and tension.
3. Sleep: A consistent sleep schedule with 7-9 hours of sleep per night is essential for cognitive function, emotional well-being, and stress management.

B. Tips for Healthy Lifestyle Choices

1. Balanced Diet: Encourage teenagers to consume a variety of nutritious foods and limit the intake of sugary and processed foods.
2. Regular Exercise: Engaging in physical activities they enjoy, whether it's sports, dancing, or hiking, can boost mood and reduce stress.
3. Adequate Sleep: Establishing a bedtime routine and limiting screen time before sleep can promote better sleep quality.

IV. Emotional Expression

Effective emotional expression is vital for teenagers to manage stress and maintain mental well-being. Encouraging teenagers to understand and express their feelings and seek support when needed is essential.

A. The Importance of Emotional Expression

   1. Preventing Bottling-Up Emotions: Suppressing emotions can lead to increased stress and anxiety. Encouraging teenagers to express their feelings helps prevent emotional buildup.
   2. Seeking Support: Teenagers should be encouraged to reach out to friends, family, or professionals when they're struggling emotionally. Sharing their feelings can provide valuable insight and support.

B. Promoting Healthy Emotional Expression

   1. Journaling: Keeping a journal allows teenagers to process their emotions and gain clarity on their feelings and thoughts.
   2. Effective Communication: Teach teenagers effective communication skills to express their feelings, needs, and concerns in a constructive manner.
   3. Therapeutic Support: When necessary, consider seeking the assistance of a mental health professional who can provide guidance and support for emotional challenges.

V. Relaxation Techniques

Relaxation exercises can calm the mind and body, reducing stress and promoting a sense of peace and well-being.

Teenagers can benefit greatly from incorporating relaxation techniques into their daily routines.

A. Progressive Muscle Relaxation
    1. The Technique: Progressive muscle relaxation involves systematically tensing and then relaxing different muscle groups in the body. This helps relieve physical tension and promotes relaxation.
    2. How to Practice: Teenagers can start by sitting or lying down in a comfortable position. They then focus on one muscle group at a time, tensing it for a few seconds and then relaxing it completely. They work their way through the entire body, from head to toe.
B. Guided Imagery
    1. The Technique: Guided imagery involves using your imagination to create calming and peaceful mental images. This technique can help reduce stress and anxiety.
    2. How to Practice: Teenagers can find guided imagery exercises online or through apps. They listen to a recorded guide who takes them through a calming and peaceful mental journey, such as imagining a serene beach or a tranquil forest.

VI. Coping Skills

Coping skills are strategies that teenagers can use in the moment to deal with stress and anxiety. These techniques help them manage their emotions and reduce the impact of stressors.

A. Deep Breathing
   1. The Technique: Deep breathing involves taking slow, deep breaths to calm the body's stress response and reduce anxiety.
   2. How to Practice: Teenagers can practice deep breathing by taking a deep breath in through their nose, holding it for a few seconds, and then exhaling slowly through their mouth. This can be repeated several times until they feel more relaxed.
B. Positive Self-Talk
   1. The Technique: Positive self-talk involves replacing negative or self-critical thoughts with more positive and encouraging ones.
   2. How to Practice: Encourage teenagers to identify negative thoughts and challenge them. For example, if they're thinking, "I'll never succeed at this," they can replace it with, "I'll do my best, and that's what matters."

C. Stress Reduction Techniques
   1. The Technique: Stress reduction techniques can include engaging in hobbies, spending time with loved ones, or engaging in activities that bring joy and relaxation.
   2. How to Practice: Teenagers should identify activities that help them relax and make time for them in their daily lives. Whether it's reading, listening to music, or engaging in creative pursuits, these activities can provide an essential outlet for stress.

Teenagers face a range of challenges in their lives that can lead to stress and anxiety. However, by incorporating the six key strategies discussed in this guide - Mindfulness and Meditation, Time Management, Healthy Lifestyle Choices, Emotional Expression, Relaxation Techniques, and Coping Skills - they can empower themselves to take control of their mental and emotional well-being.

These practices are not standalone solutions but work synergistically to provide a comprehensive approach to managing stress. Encourage teenagers to explore and integrate these techniques into their daily routines to promote resilience, reduce stress, and foster a positive and balanced life.

It's also important to remind teenagers that seeking professional help, when necessary, is a crucial part of managing stress and anxiety. If their stress becomes overwhelming or persistent, a mental health professional can provide expert guidance and support. By combining these self-help techniques with professional assistance when needed, teenagers can navigate the challenges of adolescence with greater confidence and well-being.

In this chapter, we've explored the stressors that commonly affect teenagers, effective stress-reduction techniques, and inspiring stories of success. By understanding stress, developing coping strategies, and seeking support when needed, you can navigate the challenges of teenage life with resilience and confidence. Remember that managing stress is a skill that you can develop over time, and it's an essential part of your personal growth journey.

Chapter 3: Battling Depression

Depression is a serious and often misunderstood mental health condition that affects millions of teenagers worldwide. In this comprehensive chapter, we will delve deep into the topic of depression, exploring the signs and symptoms, the importance of seeking help and support, and real-life stories of triumph over this challenging condition. By understanding depression and learning how to manage it, you can take the first steps toward healing and reclaiming your life.

Section 1: Signs of Depression

Recognizing the Darkness Within

Depression is more than just feeling sad; it's a complex emotional and psychological condition that can significantly impact your life. In this section, we will explore the signs and symptoms of depression, including:

- Persistent Sadness: Understanding the difference between normal sadness and chronic, unexplained feelings of sadness.
- Loss of Interest: How depression can steal away your enthusiasm and interest in activities you once enjoyed.
- Changes in Appetite and Sleep: Exploring how depression can affect your eating and sleeping patterns.

- Fatigue and Low Energy: The overwhelming sense of exhaustion that often accompanies depression.
- Feelings of Hopelessness: The sense that things will never get better, even when there is hope.
- Difficulty Concentrating: The cognitive challenges that depression can bring.
- Physical Symptoms: How depression can manifest physically, including headaches and body aches.

Overcoming Teenage Depression: Strategies for Healing and Resilience

Teenage depression is a challenging and complex mental health issue that can significantly impact an individual's life. While it's essential to recognize the symptoms of depression, it's equally crucial to understand that there are strategies and interventions that can help teenagers address and overcome these challenges. In this comprehensive guide, we will explore practical approaches for teenagers to address each of the common problems associated with depression. By understanding these issues and learning effective coping mechanisms, teenagers can regain control of their mental well-being and embark on a path towards healing and resilience.

I. Addressing Persistent Sadness

Persistent sadness is a hallmark symptom of depression. Understanding the difference between normal sadness and chronic, unexplained feelings of sadness is the first step in addressing this issue.

A. Recognizing Normal Sadness vs. Depression

   1. Normal Sadness: Sadness is a natural human emotion that occurs in response to specific events, such as a breakup, a loss, or a disappointing experience. It is temporary and often proportional to the situation.
   2. Chronic Sadness (Depression): Depression involves a persistent and unexplained feeling of extreme sadness and despair that lasts for an extended period, often weeks, months, or even years, and is not directly linked to a particular event or circumstance.

B. Strategies for Addressing Persistent Sadness

   1. Talk About Your Feelings: Opening up to a trusted friend, family member, or therapist can provide an outlet for expressing your emotions and gaining support.
   2. Engage in Creative Expression: Creative activities like art, writing, or music can be powerful ways to process and release feelings of sadness.
   3. Seek Professional Help: If your persistent sadness is interfering with your daily life and well-being, consider consulting a mental health professional who can provide therapy and support.

II. Regaining Lost Interests

Loss of interest in activities that once brought joy and fulfilment can be a challenging aspect of teenage depression. To address this problem, it's important to gradually reintroduce enjoyable activities into your life.

A. Strategies for Regaining Lost Interests

1. Set Small Goals: Start by setting achievable, small goals related to activities you once enjoyed. This can help you build motivation and regain a sense of accomplishment.
2. Try New Activities: Explore new hobbies or activities that you may not have tried before. Sometimes, discovering new interests can be a refreshing experience.
3. Spend Time with Supportive Friends: Surround yourself with friends who are understanding and supportive. Socializing with friends can motivate you to engage in activities you used to enjoy.
4. Gradual Reintroduction: Don't rush the process. Understand that it's okay to take small steps towards rekindling your interests, and it's normal for progress to be gradual.

III. Managing Changes in Appetite and Sleep

Depression can disrupt eating and sleeping patterns. Addressing these changes is essential for physical well-being and overall mental health.

A. Strategies for Managing Changes in Appetite and Sleep

1. Establish Routine: Create a daily schedule that includes regular meal times and a consistent sleep schedule. Maintaining a routine can help stabilize your appetite and improve sleep.
2. Balanced Diet: Focus on eating a balanced diet with plenty of fruits, vegetables, lean proteins, and whole grains. Avoid excessive consumption of sugary or processed foods.
3. Physical Activity: Engaging in regular physical activity can improve sleep quality and appetite regulation. Aim for at least 30 minutes of exercise most days of the week.
4. Limit Caffeine and Screen Time: Reduce caffeine intake, especially in the afternoon and evening, and limit screen time before bedtime to improve sleep quality.
5. Stress Reduction Techniques: Incorporate relaxation techniques, such as deep breathing exercises or mindfulness meditation, into your daily routine to manage stress, which can impact appetite and sleep.

IV. Combating Fatigue and Low Energy

Fatigue and low energy are common symptoms of depression that can be overwhelming. However, there are strategies to combat these feelings and regain vitality.

A. Strategies for Combating Fatigue and Low Energy

1. Physical Activity: Engage in regular physical activity, as it can boost energy levels and improve mood. Even a short walk can make a significant difference.
2. Adequate Sleep: Prioritize sleep hygiene by creating a comfortable sleep environment, maintaining a consistent sleep schedule, and practicing relaxation techniques before bed.
3. Nutritious Diet: Consume a balanced diet that provides the essential nutrients your body needs for energy. Avoid excessive sugar and processed foods, as they can lead to energy crashes.
4. Break Tasks into Smaller Steps: When faced with tasks that seem overwhelming, break them down into smaller, manageable steps. Completing each step can provide a sense of accomplishment and increase motivation.
5. Prioritize Self-Care: Take time for self-care activities that recharge your physical and emotional well-being, such as reading, taking a bath, or practicing relaxation exercises.

V. Cultivating Hope

Feelings of hopelessness can be pervasive in depression, but it's essential to recognize that there is hope for recovery. Cultivating hope involves adopting a more positive and realistic outlook on life.

A. Strategies for Cultivating Hope

1. Set Achievable Goals: Break down your long-term goals into smaller, achievable milestones. Celebrate your progress along the way.
2. Challenge Negative Thoughts: Practice cognitive-behavioral techniques to identify and challenge negative thought patterns that contribute to feelings of hopelessness.
3. Seek Professional Support: A mental health professional can provide therapy and guidance to help you address and overcome feelings of hopelessness.
4. Connect with Supportive People: Surround yourself with friends and family who provide encouragement and support. Sharing your feelings and experiences with others can instill a sense of hope.

VI. Enhancing Concentration and Cognitive Function

Depression can impair concentration and cognitive functioning, making it challenging to focus on tasks. Implementing strategies to enhance cognitive function is essential for academic and personal success.

A. Strategies for Enhancing Concentration
  1. Break Tasks into Smaller Steps: Divide tasks into smaller, more manageable parts to reduce feelings of overwhelm and make it easier to focus.
  2. Prioritize Tasks: Identify the most important tasks and tackle them first when your energy and concentration levels are highest.
  3. Eliminate Distractions: Create a conducive work environment by minimizing distractions such as noise, clutter, or electronic devices.
  4. Practice Mindfulness: Incorporate mindfulness meditation into your routine to improve focus and concentration.
  5. Stay Organized: Use planners, to-do lists, or digital tools to organize your tasks and deadlines, ensuring that you don't forget important commitments.

VII. Addressing Physical Symptoms

Physical symptoms, such as headaches and body aches, can manifest as a result of depression. While these symptoms can be distressing, there are strategies to address and manage them effectively.

A. Strategies for Addressing Physical Symptoms

   1. Relaxation Techniques: Engage in relaxation exercises, such as progressive muscle relaxation or deep breathing, to reduce physical tension and alleviate headaches and body aches.
   2. Stay Hydrated: Ensure you are drinking enough water throughout the day, as dehydration can exacerbate physical symptoms.
   3. Over-the-Counter Pain Relief: If headaches or body aches persist, consult a healthcare professional for appropriate over-the-counter pain relief options.
   4. Regular Exercise: Incorporate regular physical activity into your routine, as it can help relieve tension and reduce physical discomfort.
   5. Maintain Proper Posture: Pay attention to your posture while sitting or standing to minimize the physical strain that can contribute to headaches and body aches.

Teenage depression presents unique challenges, but with the right strategies and support, it is possible to address and overcome its various symptoms and effects. By understanding the difference between normal sadness and chronic depression, regaining lost interests, managing changes in appetite and sleep, combating fatigue, cultivating hope, enhancing concentration and cognitive function, and addressing physical symptoms, teenagers can take significant steps towards healing and resilience.

It's crucial for teenagers experiencing depression to reach out to a trusted adult, counselor, or mental health professional for guidance and support. Seeking professional help is a valuable step in the journey towards recovery and improved mental well-being. Additionally, having a strong support network of friends and family can make a significant difference in the recovery process.

Remember that healing from depression is a journey, and progress may be gradual. Be patient with yourself and celebrate even small victories along the way. With perseverance, support, and the right strategies, teenagers can overcome the challenges of depression and build a brighter future

By understanding these signs, you can recognize when depression may be affecting you or someone you care about.

Section 2: Seeking Help and Support

The Path to Healing

Depression is a treatable condition, and seeking help and support is a critical step toward recovery. In this section, we will explore the importance of reaching out for assistance, including:

- Talking to Trusted Individuals: How to open up to friends, family, or mentors about your feelings.
- Professional Help: The role of therapists, counsellors, and mental health professionals in treating depression.
- Medication: An overview of medication as a potential treatment option and what to expect.
- Self-Help Strategies: Practical strategies you can implement on your own, such as self-care, journaling, and mindfulness.
- Support Groups: The benefits of connecting with others who have experienced depression.
- Creating a Support Network: Building a network of people who are there for you during your journey.

Teenagers and Depression: Seeking Help and Building Support

Teenage depression is a complex and challenging mental health issue that can have a profound impact on a young person's life. While understanding and coping with the symptoms of depression is crucial, it is equally important to recognize that seeking help and building a strong support network are essential components of the healing process. In this comprehensive guide, we will explore various strategies and resources available to teenagers dealing with depression. From talking to trusted individuals, seeking professional help, considering medication, and implementing self-help strategies to connecting with support groups and creating a robust support network, we will provide a comprehensive roadmap to assist teenagers in their journey toward improved mental well-being.

I. Talking to Trusted Individuals

Opening up to trusted individuals, such as friends, family, or mentors, about your feelings is a critical first step in seeking help for depression. However, it can be challenging to initiate these conversations, especially when dealing with the stigma associated with mental health issues.

A. Overcoming the Stigma

1. Understanding the Stigma: Recognize that depression is a medical condition, not a sign of weakness or a character flaw. The stigma surrounding mental health can deter people from seeking help, but acknowledging its unjust nature can empower you to take action.
2. Educate Yourself: Learn about depression and its prevalence. Understanding that millions of people, including teenagers, face similar challenges can reduce the sense of isolation and stigma.
3. Challenge Negative Beliefs: Work on challenging negative beliefs or misconceptions about depression that may be contributing to self-stigma. Recognize that seeking help is a courageous and responsible step.

B. Opening Up to Trusted Individuals
   1. Choose the Right Time and Place: Find a quiet and comfortable setting where you can have an uninterrupted conversation. Choose a time when both you and the person you're confiding in are relaxed and focused.
   2. Be Honest and Open: Express your feelings honestly, explaining what you've been going through, how it has affected you, and what kind of support you need. It's okay to be vulnerable and share your struggles.
   3. Use "I" Statements: Frame your thoughts and emotions using "I" statements to express your feelings without making others defensive. For example, say, "I have been feeling really sad and overwhelmed lately," instead of "You make me sad."
   4. Provide Information: Offer information about depression, including its symptoms, so that your trusted individual can better understand what you're experiencing.
   5. Set Realistic Expectations: Recognize that the person you confide in may not fully understand or know how to respond. Be patient and allow them to process the information.

II. Professional Help

While talking to trusted individuals can provide valuable emotional support, professional help is often necessary to effectively treat depression. Therapists, counsellors, and mental health professionals play a crucial role in diagnosing and treating depression.

A. The Role of Therapists and Counsellors

   1. Therapy Options: Therapists and counsellors offer a variety of therapeutic approaches, such as cognitive-behavioural therapy (CBT), dialectical behaviour therapy (DBT), and interpersonal therapy (IPT). These approaches can help teenagers address the underlying causes of depression and develop coping strategies.
   2. Individualized Treatment: Therapists work with teenagers to create personalized treatment plans tailored to their unique needs and circumstances.
   3. Safe and Confidential Environment: Therapy provides a safe and confidential space for teenagers to express their thoughts and feelings without judgment.

B. What to Expect from Professional Help

   1. Assessment: In the initial sessions, the therapist will assess the severity and nature of your depression. They may ask questions about your symptoms, life experiences, and family history.
   2. Treatment Plan: After the assessment, the therapist will work with you to develop a treatment

plan, which may include individual therapy, group therapy, or a combination of approaches.
3. Therapeutic Techniques: Therapists will employ various therapeutic techniques to help you manage depression, improve coping skills, challenge negative thought patterns, and set achievable goals.
4. Regular Sessions: Therapy typically involves regular sessions, ranging from weekly to monthly, depending on your needs and progress.
5. Medication Consultation: In some cases, therapists may recommend consulting a psychiatrist for a medication evaluation. Medication can be an effective component of treatment for moderate to severe depression.

III. Medication

Medication can be a valuable tool in treating depression, particularly when symptoms are severe or do not respond well to therapy alone. However, medication should always be prescribed and monitored by a qualified healthcare professional.

A. Medication Options

1. Antidepressants: Antidepressant medications, such as selective serotonin reuptake inhibitors (SSRIs) or serotonin-norepinephrine reuptake inhibitors (SNRIs), can help regulate brain chemistry and alleviate depressive symptoms.

2. Mood Stabilizers: In some cases, mood stabilizers or atypical antipsychotic medications may be prescribed to manage depression, especially when there are mood fluctuations or psychosis present.

B. What to Expect from Medication

1. Evaluation and Diagnosis: Before prescribing medication, a psychiatrist will evaluate your symptoms, diagnose depression, and determine the most appropriate treatment plan.
2. Medication Adjustments: Finding the right medication and dosage may require some adjustments. It's essential to communicate openly with your psychiatrist about any side effects or changes in your symptoms.
3. Regular Monitoring: While taking medication, you will have regular follow-up appointments with your psychiatrist to assess your progress and ensure that the medication is effective and well-tolerated.
4. Complementary Therapy: Medication is often used in conjunction with therapy to provide comprehensive treatment for depression.

IV. Self-Help Strategies

In addition to seeking professional help, teenagers can implement self-help strategies to manage and alleviate depression symptoms. These strategies are valuable tools that can be integrated into daily life.

A. Self-Care Practices
   1. Healthy Lifestyle: Focus on maintaining a balanced diet, regular exercise, and adequate sleep. Physical health and mental well-being are closely interconnected.
   2. Mindfulness and Meditation: Practice mindfulness exercises and meditation to reduce stress, manage negative thoughts, and stay grounded in the present moment.
   3. Journaling: Keep a journal to express your thoughts and emotions. Journaling can provide clarity, help identify triggers, and track progress.
   4. Relaxation Techniques: Engage in relaxation exercises, such as deep breathing, progressive muscle relaxation, or guided imagery, to alleviate physical tension and promote relaxation.

B. Positive Self-Talk
   1. Challenge Negative Thoughts: Identify and challenge negative thought patterns, such as self-criticism or catastrophic thinking. Replace them with more positive and realistic thoughts.
   2. Affirmations: Create positive affirmations that promote self-worth and resilience. Repeat these affirmations regularly to reinforce a positive self-image.
   3. Self-Compassion: Practice self-compassion by treating yourself with the same kindness and

understanding that you would offer to a friend facing similar challenges.

C. Time Management and Goal Setting

1. Prioritize Tasks: Use time management techniques, such as creating to-do lists or using productivity apps, to prioritize tasks and manage responsibilities effectively.
2. Set Achievable Goals: Break down larger goals into smaller, more manageable steps. Setting achievable goals can provide a sense of accomplishment and motivation.
3. Establish Routine: Create a daily routine that includes regular sleep patterns, meal times, and designated study or work periods.

D. Seek Pleasure and Connection

1. Engage in Enjoyable Activities: Make an effort to engage in activities you once enjoyed, even if you don't initially feel like it. Doing so can boost your mood and motivation.
2. Connect with Supportive People: Maintain connections with friends and family who provide emotional support. Social interaction is crucial for mental well-being.

V. Support Groups

Support groups provide a unique and valuable resource for teenagers dealing with depression. These groups offer a sense of community, understanding, and shared experiences.

A. Benefits of Support Groups

   1. Reduced Isolation: Support groups help combat feelings of isolation by connecting teenagers with others who have experienced similar struggles.
   2. Validation: Sharing experiences and emotions in a group setting can validate your feelings and provide a sense of belonging.
   3. Shared Coping Strategies: Support groups offer a platform for members to share coping strategies and tips for managing depression effectively.
   4. Encouragement: Group members can provide encouragement, motivation, and hope through their own stories of recovery and progress.

B. Finding a Support Group

   1. Local Resources: Check with local mental health organizations, schools, or community centres for information on support groups in your area.
   2. Online Support Groups: Online support groups and forums provide a convenient way to connect with others facing depression, especially if you prefer anonymity.

3. Themed Groups: Some support groups focus on specific aspects of depression, such as teen depression, anxiety, or grief. Consider your specific needs when seeking a group.

VI. Creating a Support Network

Building a robust support network is essential for managing depression effectively. Your support network may include friends, family members, mentors, and professionals who play a vital role in your journey towards improved mental well-being.

A. Identify Your Supportive Individuals
   1. Trusted Friends: Identify friends who are empathetic, non-judgmental, and willing to listen. These friends can provide emotional support when needed.
   2. Family Members: Communicate with family members about your needs and the type of support you require. Encourage open dialogue about depression within your family.
   3. Mentors and Teachers: Teachers, coaches, or mentors at school or in extracurricular activities can be valuable sources of guidance and support.
   4. Therapists and Counsellors: Establish a trusting and open relationship with your therapist or counsellor. They are there to provide professional guidance and support.

B. Communicate Your Needs
   1. Express Your Needs: Clearly communicate your needs to your support network. Let them know how they can best support you, whether it's through active listening, encouragement, or specific actions.
   2. Encourage Open Dialogue: Encourage open and honest communication within your support network. Express your feelings and experiences, and encourage others to do the same.
   3. Set Boundaries: Establish boundaries when necessary to protect your mental well-being. Let your support network know when you need space or time for self-care.
   4. Regular Check-Ins: Maintain regular check-ins with your support network to keep them updated on your progress and challenges.

Teenagers dealing with depression face a unique set of challenges, but seeking help and building a strong support network are essential steps in the path toward recovery and improved mental well-being. From talking to trusted individuals and seeking professional help to considering medication, implementing self-help strategies, connecting with support groups, and creating a robust support network, teenagers have a range of resources and strategies at their disposal.

Remember that seeking help is a sign of strength, not weakness. It takes courage to open up about your feelings and take proactive steps toward healing. By combining the support of trusted individuals with professional guidance, self-help strategies, and the connections formed through support groups, teenagers can effectively manage depression and work towards a brighter and healthier future

By seeking help and support, you're not only taking control of your mental health but also opening the door to healing and recovery.

By the end of this chapter, you will have a comprehensive understanding of depression, its signs and symptoms, and the crucial steps to take when seeking help and support. The real-life stories of triumph over depression will inspire and reassure you that recovery is possible. Remember, you are not alone in this journey, and there is hope for a brighter, happier tomorrow

CHAPTER 4: Navigating the Social Media Maze

In today's digital age, social media has become an integral part of teenage life. It offers numerous benefits and opportunities for connection and self-expression, but it also comes with its own set of challenges and potential pitfalls. In this comprehensive chapter, we will explore the world of social media, examining both its advantages and drawbacks. We will also provide guidance on how to establish healthy online boundaries.

Section 1: Benefits and Pitfalls of Social Media

The Double-Edged Sword

Social media has revolutionized the way we communicate and connect with others, but it's essential to recognize both its benefits and pitfalls, including:

- Advantages of Social Media: Exploring how social media can foster friendships, provide opportunities for self-expression, and serve as a valuable source of information and entertainment.
- Drawbacks of Social Media: Discussing the potential negative impacts of excessive screen time, cyberbullying, social comparison, and the erosion of privacy.

- Impact on Mental Health: Examining the complex relationship between social media use and mental well-being, including the potential for anxiety and depression.
- Digital Detox: Strategies for taking breaks from social media to promote better mental health and reduce the negative effects of overuse.

Navigating the Digital Landscape: Social Media and Teenagers

Introduction

In today's digital age, social media has become an integral part of the lives of teenagers. With the rise of platforms like Facebook, Instagram, Twitter, Snapchat, and TikTok, adolescents have more ways than ever to connect, express themselves, and access information and entertainment. While social media offers numerous advantages, it also poses significant challenges and potential drawbacks that can affect the mental health and well-being of teenagers. In this comprehensive guide, we will explore the complex terrain of social media for teenagers, delving into the advantages, drawbacks, impact on mental health, and strategies for a healthy digital detox.

I. Advantages of Social Media

Social media platforms offer a range of advantages for teenagers, enriching their lives in various ways:

A. Fostering Friendships

    1. Connectivity: Social media enables teenagers to stay connected with friends and family, regardless of geographic distance, fostering a sense of closeness and community.
    2. Expanding Social Circles: Teens can expand their social circles by making new friends online who share common interests and experiences.
    3. Maintaining Relationships: Social media provides a convenient means for maintaining relationships, especially in a fast-paced world where in-person interactions may be limited.

B. Opportunities for Self-Expression

    1. Creative Outlets: Platforms like Instagram and TikTok offer creative outlets for self-expression through photos, videos, and artistic content.
    2. Voice and Advocacy: Teenagers can use social media to amplify their voices and advocate for causes they care about, promoting social change and awareness.

C. Valuable Source of Information

    1. Educational Resources: Social media platforms serve as valuable educational resources, offering access to a wealth of information, news, and articles on a wide range of topics.

2. Real-Time Updates: Users can stay updated on current events, trends, and developments in various fields, helping them stay informed and engaged.

D. Entertainment and Leisure
   1. Entertainment: Social media platforms are a source of entertainment, providing access to a vast array of videos, memes, and games.
   2. Community Engagement: Teenagers can engage with fan communities, sharing their passion for music, movies, and other interests.

II. Drawbacks of Social Media

While social media offers numerous advantages, it is not without its drawbacks, which can have a significant impact on teenagers:

A. Excessive Screen Time
   1. Digital Addiction: Excessive use of social media can lead to digital addiction, which can interfere with academic performance, physical health, and overall well-being.
   2. Sleep Disruption: Prolonged screen time, especially before bedtime, can disrupt sleep patterns and contribute to sleep-related problems.

B. Cyberbullying
   1. Online Harassment: Social media platforms can become platforms for cyberbullying, where teenagers may experience harassment, threats, or exclusion from peers.
   2. Mental Health Effects: Cyberbullying can have severe mental health effects, leading to anxiety, depression, and even suicidal thoughts in some cases.
C. Social Comparison
   1. Highlight Reel Effect: Social media often presents a curated version of reality, creating a "highlight reel" effect where users compare their lives to others' seemingly perfect lives.
   2. Negative Self-Image: Constant social comparison can lead to negative self-image, low self-esteem, and body dissatisfaction.
D. Erosion of Privacy
   1. Data Privacy Concerns: Social media platforms collect vast amounts of user data, raising concerns about privacy and data security.
   2. Online Reputation: Inappropriate posts or actions on social media can have long-lasting consequences, affecting a teenager's online reputation and future opportunities.

III. Impact on Mental Health

The relationship between social media use and mental health among teenagers is complex, with both positive and negative effects:

A. Positive Impact
 1. Connection: Social media can provide a sense of connection and support, reducing feelings of isolation and loneliness.
 2. Awareness and Education: Platforms can raise awareness about mental health issues and provide educational resources on coping strategies and seeking help.

B. Negative Impact
 1. Anxiety and Depression: Excessive social media use, especially when associated with cyberbullying and social comparison, can contribute to anxiety and depression.
 2. Fear of Missing Out (FOMO): FOMO, a phenomenon fueled by social media, can lead to anxiety and stress.
 3. Negative Body Image: Constant exposure to idealized body images on social media can contribute to body dissatisfaction and eating disorders.

IV. Digital Detox

Recognizing the potential drawbacks and their impact on mental health, teenagers can benefit from strategies for taking breaks from social media, often referred to as a "digital detox."

A. Setting Boundaries
   1. Screen-Free Zones: Designate areas in your home, such as the bedroom, as screen-free zones to promote healthier sleep habits.
   2. Scheduled Screen Time: Set specific times for social media use and adhere to those schedules.
   3. Notifications: Disable non-essential notifications to reduce the impulse to check your phone constantly.

B. Exploring Offline Activities
   1. Hobbies: Engage in offline hobbies and interests that provide enjoyment and fulfillment.
   2. Physical Activity: Exercise is a great way to promote mental well-being and reduce screen time.
   3. Reading: Spend time reading books, magazines, or articles to broaden your knowledge and stimulate your mind.

C. Mindfulness and Self-Care
   1. Mindfulness Practices: Incorporate mindfulness meditation or relaxation techniques into your daily routine to manage stress and reduce anxiety.

2. Self-Care: Prioritize self-care activities, such as taking baths, practicing deep breathing exercises, or journaling, to maintain mental and emotional well-being.

D. Social Media Cleanse
1. Delete Apps: Temporarily delete social media apps from your devices to create distance and reduce the temptation to use them.
2. Unfollow or Mute: Unfollow accounts that negatively impact your mental health or cause comparison. Mute keywords or phrases related to mental health triggers.
3. Evaluate Your Feed: Curate your social media feed by following accounts that promote positivity, mental health awareness, and self-acceptance.

E. Seek Professional Help
1. Consult a Therapist: If you find it challenging to reduce or control your social media use, consider consulting a therapist who specializes in digital addiction or behavioral issues.
2. Online Support: Online communities and mental health apps can also provide support for those seeking a digital detox.

V. Balancing Social Media Use

The key to a healthy relationship with social media is balance. Recognize the advantages and drawbacks, and take proactive steps to manage your social media use effectively:

A. Practice Mindful Consumption
   1. Intentional Use: Before opening a social media app, ask yourself why you're doing it. Are you seeking connection, information, or entertainment?
   2. Monitor Emotions: Pay attention to how social media makes you feel. If you notice negative emotions, consider taking a break.

B. Limit Comparisons
   1. Focus on Real Life: Remind yourself that social media represents a curated version of reality and doesn't capture the full spectrum of people's lives.
   2. Unfollow or Hide: Unfollow accounts that trigger feelings of inadequacy or comparison.

C. Cultivate Real-Life Connections
   1. Face-to-Face Interactions: Invest time in face-to-face interactions with friends, family, and peers to foster deeper connections.
   2. Quality Over Quantity: Prioritize meaningful connections over accumulating a large number of online friends or followers.

OWL STRETCHING AND OTHER ISSUES...

D. Seek Help When Needed

   1. Professional Guidance: If you experience symptoms of anxiety, depression, or digital addiction, seek professional help. Therapists can provide guidance and strategies for managing these issues.

Navigating the digital landscape of social media as a teenager is a multifaceted journey. While social media offers undeniable advantages, it also presents challenges that can affect mental health and well-being. By understanding the advantages and drawbacks, recognizing the impact on mental health, and implementing strategies for a healthy digital detox, teenagers can find a balanced approach to social media use.

Remember that social media is a tool, and its effects on mental health can vary from person to person. It's essential to prioritize self-care, seek professional help when needed, and maintain a healthy balance between the digital and real worlds. With mindfulness and thoughtful management, teenagers can harness the advantages of social media while mitigating its potential drawbacks, ultimately leading to a healthier and more fulfilling online experience

Section 2: Establishing Healthy Online Boundaries

Finding Balance in the Digital World

Maintaining healthy online boundaries is crucial for a positive social media experience. In this section, we will explore strategies for establishing and maintaining these boundaries, including:

- Screen Time Management: Tips for setting limits on daily screen time and balancing online and offline activities.
- Privacy and Security: Guidelines for safeguarding personal information and protecting against online threats.
- Cyberbullying Prevention: Strategies for recognizing and responding to cyberbullying, as well as fostering a respectful online community.
- Healthy Comparison: Techniques for managing social comparison and maintaining a positive self-image in the digital age.

Empowering Teenagers in the Digital Age: Strategies for Screen Time Management, Privacy, Cyberbullying Prevention, and Healthy Comparison

The advent of technology has transformed the lives of teenagers, offering them a world of opportunities and challenges. While digital devices and online platforms provide unprecedented access to information, entertainment, and social connections, they also bring potential pitfalls like excessive screen time, privacy concerns, cyberbullying, and the negative effects of social comparison. In this comprehensive guide, we will explore essential techniques and strategies for teenagers to navigate the digital landscape safely and responsibly. From managing screen time and safeguarding privacy to preventing cyberbullying and fostering healthy self-image, this guide aims to empower teenagers to make informed and confident choices in their digital lives.

I. Screen Time Management

Managing screen time effectively is crucial for teenagers' physical and mental well-being. Balancing online and offline activities promotes healthier habits and helps mitigate the negative effects of excessive screen time.

A. Setting Screen Time Limits
   1. Daily Allocation: Allocate a specific amount of time for screen use each day. This can help create boundaries and prevent excessive use.
   2. Breaks Between Activities: Incorporate short breaks between screen-based activities to rest your eyes, stretch, and engage in other activities.
   3. Use of Timers: Utilize timer apps or built-in device features to set time limits for specific apps or activities.

B. Prioritizing Offline Activities
   1. Hobbies and Interests: Dedicate time to offline hobbies and interests, such as sports, art, reading, or playing a musical instrument.

2. Physical Activity: Regular physical activity is essential for overall health. Schedule time for exercise or outdoor activities.
3. Socializing: Spend time with friends and family in face-to-face interactions. Building and maintaining real-life relationships is vital.

C. Creating a Technology-Free Zone
1. Bedroom Boundaries: Keep digital devices out of the bedroom to promote better sleep and prevent late-night screen time.
2. Designated Screen Areas: Designate specific areas of your home for screen use, such as a home office or living room, to avoid distractions in other spaces.
3. Device-Free Meals: Make mealtimes device-free to encourage meaningful conversations and mindful eating.

D. Monitoring Screen Time
1. Parental Control Tools: If necessary, use parental control apps or tools that allow parents to monitor and set limits on screen time.
2. Self-Monitoring: Keep a log of your screen time to raise awareness of your usage patterns and identify areas for improvement.

II. Privacy and Security

Protecting personal information and staying safe online is a critical aspect of responsible digital citizenship. Teenagers should be aware of privacy risks and take steps to safeguard their online presence.

A. Safeguarding Personal Information

1. Strong Passwords: Use strong, unique passwords for online accounts, and consider using a reputable password manager to keep track of them.
2. Two-Factor Authentication (2FA): Enable 2FA whenever possible to add an extra layer of security to your online accounts.
3. Limit Sharing: Be cautious about sharing personal information like your full name, address, phone number, and school on social media or public forums.

B. Social Media Privacy Settings

1. Review Privacy Settings: Regularly review and adjust the privacy settings on your social media profiles to control who can see your posts and personal information.
2. Limit Friend Requests: Only accept friend requests or follow requests from people you know and trust.
3. Be Cautious with Location Sharing: Avoid sharing your real-time location on social media apps, especially with strangers.

C. Recognizing Online Threats

   1. Phishing Awareness: Be cautious of suspicious emails, messages, or links, and avoid clicking on them. Educate yourself about phishing techniques.
   2. Online Predators: Be vigilant when interacting with strangers online, especially in gaming communities or chat rooms. Never share personal information or arrange in-person meetings with someone you met online.

D. Reporting Abuse

   1. Cyberbullying: If you experience cyberbullying or witness it happening to someone else, report it to the platform or social media site and seek support from a trusted adult.
   2. Online Harassment: Report online harassment, threats, or hate speech to the platform's moderators or administrators. Document evidence if necessary.

III. Cyberbullying Prevention

Cyberbullying is a significant concern in the digital age, and teenagers should be equipped with strategies to recognize, prevent, and respond to this form of harassment.

A. Identifying Cyberbullying

   1. Types of Cyberbullying: Familiarize yourself with the various forms of cyberbullying, which may

include harassment, impersonation, exclusion, or sharing harmful content.
2. Gut Feeling: Trust your instincts. If something feels hurtful or inappropriate online, it may be a form of cyberbullying.

B. Responding to Cyberbullying

1. Don't Engage: Avoid responding to cyberbullies, as engaging with them can escalate the situation. Block or mute the person if possible.
2. Document Evidence: Keep records of abusive messages or posts as evidence, including screenshots and timestamps.
3. Report to Authorities: If the cyberbullying involves threats, harassment, or illegal activity, report it to the relevant authorities or law enforcement.

C. Seeking Support

1. Talk to Someone: Reach out to a trusted adult, such as a parent, teacher, school counsellor, or coach, and share your experience.
2. Mental Health Support: If cyberbullying is affecting your mental health, consider seeking support from a therapist or counsellor to help cope with the emotional impact.

IV. Healthy Comparison

Social media often fosters an environment of comparison, where individuals compare their lives to others, potentially leading to negative self-image and self-esteem issues. Implementing techniques to manage healthy comparison is crucial.

A. Recognizing Unrealistic Expectations
   1. Highlight Reel vs. Reality: Remember that what you see on social media is often a curated "highlight reel" of someone's life, not the full picture.
   2. Filters and Editing: Understand that filters, photo editing, and retouching can significantly alter the way people appear in photos online.

B. Limiting Exposure
   1. Unfollow Negative Influences: Unfollow or mute accounts that consistently trigger feelings of inadequacy or comparison.
   2. Limit Exposure: Reduce the time spent on platforms that tend to foster unhealthy comparison.

C. Building a Positive Self-Image
   1. Positive Affirmations: Practice positive self-talk and affirmations to boost self-esteem and self-worth.
   2. Focus on Personal Growth: Shift your focus from external validation to personal growth and self-improvement.

3. Seek Support: Reach out to friends, family, or professionals if you struggle with self-esteem issues or negative self-image.

As teenagers navigate the digital landscape, they encounter numerous opportunities and challenges. Techniques for effective screen time management, safeguarding privacy and security, preventing cyberbullying, and managing healthy comparison are essential skills for responsible digital citizenship. By implementing these strategies, teenagers can harness the benefits of technology while minimizing potential risks and protecting their physical and mental well-being.

Remember that responsible digital behaviour and online safety are ongoing commitments. Stay informed about emerging digital trends and potential threats, and continue to prioritize your personal growth, well-being, and healthy relationships in both the digital and real world. Empower yourself to make informed and responsible choices as you navigate the exciting and ever-evolving digital age

Part II

Interpersonal Relationships

In this section of our comprehensive guide, we'll delve deep into the complex world of interpersonal relationships, tackling three critical topics that many teenagers encounter: confronting bullying, addressing eating disorders and body image issues, and understanding and dealing with peer pressure.

Chapter 5: Confronting Bullying

Bullying is a pervasive issue in today's society, and it affects countless teenagers worldwide. This chapter will explore the different types of bullying, strategies to address and prevent bullying, and inspiring stories of resilience that showcase how individuals have overcome the challenges of being bullied.

Types of Bullying

Understanding the Forms of Bullying

Bullying can take various forms, and it's essential to recognize and understand these types to address them effectively. We'll explore:

- Physical Bullying: Instances of physical harm or aggression.
- Verbal Bullying: Hurtful words, name-calling, and insults.
- Social Bullying: Manipulation, exclusion, and spreading rumors.
- Cyberbullying: Harassment and cruelty in the digital realm.
- Sexual Bullying: Inappropriate comments or actions of a sexual nature.

- Prejudice-Based Bullying: Discrimination based on race, gender, sexuality, or other factors.

Understanding the different types of bullying is the first step in combatting this pervasive issue.

Strategies to Address and Prevent Bullying

Empowering You to Take Action

Addressing and preventing bullying requires a proactive approach. In this section, we'll discuss:

- Recognizing Bullying: Strategies to identify when bullying is occurring.
- Reporting and Seeking Help: How to report bullying incidents to authorities or trusted adults.
- Supporting Victims: Ways to provide support and encouragement to those who have been bullied.
- Bystander Intervention: The role of bystanders in preventing and stopping bullying.
- Creating a Safe Environment: The importance of fostering a culture of kindness and inclusion.

Empowering Teenagers: Strategies to Recognize, Report, and Prevent Bullying

Bullying is a pervasive issue that affects countless teenagers across the world. It can take various forms, including verbal, physical, relational, and cyberbullying, and can have severe consequences on the mental, emotional, and physical well-being of those involved. As a teenager, understanding how to recognize, report, and prevent bullying is essential for creating a safe and supportive environment for yourself and your peers. In this comprehensive guide, we will explore strategies to help teenagers address bullying effectively, covering topics such as recognizing bullying, reporting incidents, supporting victims, bystander intervention, and fostering a culture of kindness and inclusion.

I. Recognizing Bullying

Recognizing bullying is the first step in addressing the issue. It is essential to distinguish between normal conflicts or disagreements and bullying behavior:

A. Types of Bullying
   1. Verbal Bullying: Verbal bullying involves using words to hurt, demean, or intimidate others through name-calling, insults, or threats.
   2. Physical Bullying: Physical bullying includes acts of physical harm, such as hitting, pushing, or tripping others.
   3. Relational Bullying: Relational bullying focuses on damaging social relationships, often through exclusion, spreading rumors, or manipulating friendships.

4. Cyberbullying: Cyberbullying takes place online, where individuals use technology to harass, threaten, or spread harmful content about others.

B. Signs of Bullying

1. Emotional Changes: Look for signs of emotional distress, such as sudden mood swings, anxiety, or depression.
2. Physical Symptoms: Physical complaints like headaches, stomachaches, or changes in eating or sleeping patterns can indicate bullying.
3. Isolation: Victims of bullying may withdraw from social activities or lose interest in previously enjoyed activities.
4. Declining Academic Performance: Bullying can lead to a decline in academic performance, as victims may struggle to concentrate and feel safe in school.
5. Changes in Behavior: Watch for changes in behavior, such as avoidance of specific places or individuals.

C. Trust Your Instincts

1. Gut Feeling: If something feels wrong or hurtful, trust your instincts. It's better to be cautious and seek help when in doubt.
2. Speak Up: Encourage open communication with trusted adults or friends about your experiences and concerns.

II. Reporting and Seeking Help

Reporting bullying incidents is crucial for addressing the issue and ensuring the safety of those involved. Here's how teenagers can report bullying and seek assistance:

A. Reporting to Trusted Adults

1. Parents and Guardians: Share your experiences with your parents or guardians, as they can provide guidance and support in addressing the situation.
2. Teachers and School Staff: Inform teachers, school counselors, or administrators about the bullying incidents, as they have a responsibility to ensure a safe learning environment.
3. School Hotlines: Many schools have anonymous reporting hotlines or online forms that allow you to report bullying incidents discreetly.

B. Documenting Incidents

1. Keep Records: Document details of bullying incidents, including dates, times, locations, individuals involved, and descriptions of the behavior.
2. Save Evidence: If the bullying occurs online, take screenshots or save copies of harmful messages or posts as evidence.

C. Seeking Professional Help

   1. Therapist or Counselor: If you are experiencing severe emotional distress due to bullying, consider seeking support from a therapist or counselor to help cope with the emotional impact.
   2. Support Groups: Joining support groups for bullying victims can provide a sense of community and understanding.

III. Supporting Victims

Supporting victims of bullying is essential to help them cope with the emotional and psychological toll of the experience:

A. Active Listening

   1. Empathetic Listening: Be an empathetic listener by providing a safe space for the victim to express their feelings and experiences without judgment.
   2. Ask Open-Ended Questions: Encourage victims to share by asking open-ended questions that allow them to express themselves freely.

B. Encouragement and Validation

   1. Empowerment: Encourage victims to stand up for themselves and seek help from trusted adults or authorities.
   2. Validation: Validate the victim's feelings and experiences by acknowledging their pain and offering reassurance.

C. Reporting Together

1. Accompany Victims: Offer to accompany the victim when reporting bullying incidents to school authorities or other relevant parties.
2. Maintain Privacy: Respect the victim's privacy and confidentiality when discussing the situation with others.

IV. Bystander Intervention

Bystanders play a crucial role in preventing and stopping bullying. Here's how teenagers can intervene effectively:

A. Recognizing the Responsibility

1. Understand Your Role: Recognize that bystanders have the power to make a positive difference by intervening in bullying situations.
2. Avoid Being a Silent Witness: Do not ignore or remain silent when witnessing bullying. Your actions or words can make a significant impact.

B. Safe Intervention Strategies

1. Direct Intervention: If safe, directly intervene by calmly and assertively telling the bully to stop or by offering support to the victim.
2. Distract and Divert: If direct intervention is not possible, create a distraction or divert the bully's attention away from the victim.

3. Support the Victim: After the bullying incident, offer support and empathy to the victim. Encourage them to report the incident and seek help.

C. Reporting to Authorities

1. Tell an Adult: If you witness bullying and feel unable to intervene, report the incident to a trusted adult, such as a teacher or school counselor.
2. Anonymous Reporting: Many schools have anonymous reporting systems that allow bystanders to report bullying discreetly.

V. Creating a Safe Environment

Fostering a culture of kindness, empathy, and inclusion is essential for preventing bullying and ensuring a safe environment:

A. Promote Awareness

1. Educational Programs: Support and participate in educational programs and initiatives that raise awareness about bullying and its consequences.
2. Peer Workshops: Collaborate with peers to organize workshops or events that promote kindness, empathy, and conflict resolution skills.

B. Be an Ally

   1. Stand Up Against Bullying: If you witness bullying, stand up against it and support the victim. Show that you are an ally.
   2. Inclusive Attitudes: Encourage and celebrate diversity and inclusion within your school or community.

C. Encourage Reporting

   1. Reporting Channels: Advocate for clear reporting channels and encourage victims and witnesses to report bullying incidents without fear of retaliation.
   2. Support for Bystanders: Promote the idea that bystanders have a role in preventing bullying and should report incidents.

D. Supportive Peer Groups

   1. Peer Support: Establish or join peer support groups that promote kindness, empathy, and inclusivity.
   2. Anti-Bullying Clubs: Get involved in or start anti-bullying clubs within your school or community.

Addressing and preventing bullying is a collective effort that involves teenagers, adults, schools, and communities. By recognizing bullying, reporting incidents, supporting victims, intervening as bystanders, and fostering a safe and inclusive environment, teenagers can play a pivotal role in creating a world where bullying is not tolerated.

Remember that bullying is a serious issue with lasting consequences, and every teenager has the power to make a positive impact by taking a stand against it. Empower yourself and your peers to be part of the solution, and together, we can work towards a future free from bullying, where kindness and empathy prevail.

Empower yourself and others to take a stand against bullying and create a safer and more compassionate community.

Chapter 6: Eating Disorders and Body Image

Eating disorders and body image issues are pressing concerns that affect many teenagers. In this chapter, we will explore the recognition of eating disorders, the promotion of a healthy body image, and personal accounts of recovery.

Recognizing Eating Disorders

Understanding the Signs and Symptoms

Eating disorders can be challenging to identify, but early recognition is vital for intervention. We will explore:

- Anorexia Nervosa: The signs, symptoms, and risks associated with self-imposed starvation.
- Bulimia Nervosa: The cycle of binge-eating and purging, and its physical and emotional toll.
- Binge-eating disorder: Recognizing patterns of excessive eating and emotional struggles.
- Orthorexia: The obsession with healthy eating and its potential negative impact.

Understanding Eating Disorders: A Guide for Teenagers

Teenagers today face a myriad of challenges and pressures, including those related to body image, self-esteem, and societal standards of beauty. In this environment, it is essential to be aware of the signs and symptoms of eating disorders to recognize and support those who may be struggling. Eating disorders, such as Anorexia Nervosa, Bulimia Nervosa, Binge-eating disorder, and Orthorexia, can have severe physical and emotional consequences. This comprehensive guide is designed to help teenagers identify these disorders, understand their risks and effects, and provide guidance on seeking help or supporting others who may be affected.

I. Anorexia Nervosa

Anorexia Nervosa is a serious eating disorder characterized by self-imposed starvation and a distorted body image. Recognizing the signs and symptoms is essential for early intervention:

A. Physical Signs and Symptoms

1. Extreme Weight Loss: Anorexia often leads to significant and rapid weight loss, resulting in an emaciated appearance.
2. Fatigue and Weakness: A lack of essential nutrients can cause extreme fatigue, weakness, and dizziness.

3. Hair and Nail Changes: Thinning hair, brittle nails, and the development of a fine layer of body hair (lanugo) are common.
4. Cold Sensitivity: Anorexia can lead to intolerance to cold temperatures and excessive shivering.

B. Emotional and Behavioural Signs

1. Obsession with Food and Calories: Individuals with anorexia may become obsessed with calorie counting and food preparation but avoid eating.
2. Avoidance of Meals: Frequent avoidance of meals or making excuses not to eat with others is common.
3. Intense Fear of Weight Gain: An irrational and intense fear of gaining weight, despite being underweight, is a hallmark of anorexia.
4. Social Withdrawal: Anorexia can lead to social withdrawal, isolation, and a preoccupation with food and body image.

II. Bulimia Nervosa

Bulimia Nervosa is characterized by a cycle of binge-eating followed by purging behaviours, such as vomiting or excessive exercise. Recognizing this disorder involves understanding the physical and emotional toll it takes:

A. Physical Signs and Symptoms

1. Fluctuating Weight: Unlike anorexia, individuals with bulimia may maintain a relatively stable

weight, but they may experience fluctuations due to binge-purge cycles.
2. Dental Issues: Frequent vomiting can lead to dental problems, such as enamel erosion, tooth sensitivity, and cavities.
3. Swelling and Bloating: Repeated bingeing and purging can cause facial puffiness and abdominal bloating.
4. Sore Throat and Oesophageal Damage: Frequent vomiting can result in a sore throat and damage to the oesophagus.

B. Emotional and Behavioural Signs

1. Secretive Eating Habits: Those with bulimia often consume large quantities of food in secret, followed by a sense of guilt or shame.
2. Frequent Use of Laxatives or Diuretics: The use of laxatives or diuretics to control weight or compensate for binge eating is common.
3. Compulsive Exercise: Exercising excessively to burn off calories consumed during binge episodes is a key behaviour.
4. Mood Swings and Depression: Bulimia is often accompanied by mood swings, depression, and low self-esteem.

III. Binge-eating disorder

Binge-eating disorder involves recurrent episodes of excessive eating, often without the purging behaviours seen in bulimia. Recognizing this disorder requires understanding the patterns of excessive eating and the emotional struggles:

A. Physical Signs and Symptoms
   1. Weight Gain: Frequent binge eating can lead to significant weight gain and obesity-related health issues.
   2. Digestive Problems: Binge eating may result in digestive discomfort, such as bloating and indigestion.
   3. Joint Pain: Excess weight from binge eating can cause joint pain and mobility issues.
   4. Sleep Disturbances: Binge eaters may experience sleep disturbances, such as insomnia.

B. Emotional and Behavioural Signs
   1. Loss of Control: Episodes of binge eating are characterized by a sense of loss of control, as individuals consume large quantities of food in a short period.
   2. Emotional Eating: Binge eating often occurs as a response to emotional distress, such as stress, sadness, or anxiety.

3. Feelings of Guilt and Shame: Following a binge episode, individuals may experience intense feelings of guilt, shame, and regret.
4. Isolation: Binge eaters may withdraw socially due to embarrassment or shame about their eating habits.

IV. Orthorexia

Orthorexia is an eating disorder characterized by an obsession with healthy eating to the point where it becomes detrimental to physical and mental well-being. Identifying Orthorexia involves understanding the obsession with clean eating:

A. Physical Signs and Symptoms

1. Dietary Restrictions: Orthorexics impose strict dietary restrictions, often eliminating entire food groups.
2. Nutrient Deficiencies: Excessive dietary restrictions can lead to nutrient deficiencies, such as iron, calcium, or vitamin B12.
3. Extreme Exercise: Some individuals with Orthorexia may engage in excessive exercise as part of their pursuit of a "perfect" healthy lifestyle.
4. Rapid Weight Loss: In severe cases, Orthorexia can lead to rapid and unintended weight loss.

B. Emotional and Behavioural Signs
   1. Obsession with Food Quality: Orthorexics obsessively focus on the quality and purity of the food they consume, often avoiding foods they consider "impure."
   2. Social Isolation: Due to dietary restrictions, Orthorexics may isolate themselves from social gatherings or events involving food.
   3. Anxiety and Guilt: Anxiety and guilt may accompany any deviation from the strict dietary rules, even minor ones.
   4. Impact on Relationships: Orthorexia can strain relationships, as individuals may prioritize their dietary choices over social interactions.

Eating disorders are complex conditions that can have serious physical and emotional consequences for teenagers. Identifying these disorders, such as Anorexia Nervosa, Bulimia Nervosa, Binge-eating disorder, and Orthorexia, requires an understanding of their signs and symptoms, as well as their physical and emotional toll.

Recognizing the signs early and seeking help is crucial for recovery. If you or someone you know is struggling with an eating disorder, it is essential to reach out to a trusted adult, healthcare professional, or mental health specialist for support and guidance. Eating disorders are treatable, and with the right support and resources, individuals can work towards a healthier relationship with food and their bodies.

Understanding these disorders is the first step in offering support and intervention.

Promoting a Healthy Body Image

Fostering Positive Self-Perception

Body image issues are pervasive among teenagers. We will discuss:

- Media Influence: The impact of unrealistic beauty standards portrayed in media.
- Self-Esteem Building: Strategies for enhancing self-esteem and cultivating a positive self-image.
- Healthy Habits: The importance of balanced nutrition, regular exercise, and self-care.
- Supportive Environment: How friends, family, and society can contribute to a positive body image.

Navigating the Path to a Positive Body Image: A Guide for Teenagers

Teenagers today are inundated with messages about body image, beauty, and self-worth, often influenced by the media, peers, and societal pressures. It is no secret that unrealistic beauty standards portrayed in the media can negatively impact self-esteem and body image. However, teenagers have the power to develop a positive body image, cultivate self-esteem, adopt healthy habits, and create a supportive environment. In this comprehensive guide, we will explore strategies for dealing with these issues and empowering teenagers to embrace their unique selves.

I. Media Influence: Navigating Unrealistic Beauty Standards

The media plays a significant role in shaping teenagers' perceptions of beauty and body image. Understanding how media influence works is crucial for developing a healthy self-image:

A. Recognizing Media Influence

1. Deconstructing Images: Learn to deconstruct images in media by recognizing photo editing, filters, and unrealistic portrayals of beauty.
2. Filter Awareness: Understand that many social media platforms offer filters that can distort appearance. Be mindful of their effects on self-perception.
3. Diverse Representation: Advocate for diverse representation in media that showcases a range of body types, skin colours, and abilities.

B. Critical Media Consumption

   1. Media Literacy: Develop media literacy skills to discern between realistic portrayals and idealized images.
   2. Limit Exposure: Set limits on screen time and avoid media content that perpetuates unrealistic beauty standards.
   3. Choose Positive Content: Seek out media that promotes body positivity, self-acceptance, and mental well-being.

II. Self-Esteem Building: Embracing Your Unique Self

Building self-esteem is a key component of developing a positive body image. Here are strategies to enhance self-esteem and cultivate a positive self-image:

A. Self-Acceptance

   1. Practice Self-Compassion: Treat yourself with the same kindness and understanding that you offer to others.
   2. Positive Affirmations: Use positive affirmations to challenge negative self-talk and promote self-acceptance.

B. Embrace Individuality

   1. Unique Qualities: Celebrate your unique qualities, talents, and abilities that make you special.

2. Strengths and Weaknesses: Accept that everyone has strengths and weaknesses, and they contribute to your individuality.

C. Set Realistic Goals

1. Achievable Goals: Set achievable goals and celebrate your accomplishments, no matter how small.
2. Avoid Perfectionism: Recognize that perfection is unattainable and that mistakes are part of growth.

D. Seek Support

1. Talk to Trusted Adults: Share your feelings and challenges with trusted adults, such as parents, teachers, or counsellors.
2. Peer Support: Build a supportive network of friends who value and support each other's individuality.

III. Healthy Habits: Balancing Nutrition, Exercise, and Self-Care

Adopting healthy habits is essential for physical and mental well-being. These habits can contribute to a positive body image:

A. Balanced Nutrition

1. Eat Mindfully: Practice mindful eating by savouring your meals and paying attention to hunger and fullness cues.

2. Balanced Diet: Aim for a balanced diet that includes a variety of fruits, vegetables, lean proteins, and whole grains.
3. Avoid Extreme Diets: Avoid extreme diets or restrictive eating patterns that can harm your physical and mental health.

B. Regular Exercise
   1. Enjoyable Activities: Engage in physical activities that you enjoy, whether it is dancing, hiking, or team sports.
   2. Moderation: Exercise in moderation and avoid over-exercising to control weight.
   3. Focus on Health: Shift the focus of exercise from appearance to overall health and well-being.

C. Self-Care
   1. Prioritize Rest: Ensure you get enough sleep to support physical and mental health.
   2. Stress Management: Practice stress-reduction techniques such as deep breathing, meditation, or yoga.
   3. Positive Self-Talk: Replace negative self-talk with positive affirmations and self-compassion.

IV. Supportive Environment: Friends, Family, and Society

A supportive environment can significantly impact teenagers' body image and self-esteem. Here's how friends, family, and society can contribute to a positive body image:

A. Open Communication
   1. Family Discussions: Encourage open discussions about body image, self-esteem, and media influence within your family.
   2. Peer Support: Support friends who may be struggling with body image by offering a listening ear and positive reinforcement.
B. Promote Diversity
   1. Media Consumption: Be conscious of the media content you consume and seek out diverse representation.
   2. Challenge Stereotypes: Challenge stereotypes and beauty standards that perpetuate unrealistic ideals.
C. Educate and Advocate
   1. Advocate for Change: Join or support organizations and movements that promote body positivity and self-acceptance.
   2. Educational Initiatives: Advocate for educational programs in schools that address body image and self-esteem.

Developing a positive body image and self-esteem is a lifelong journey that requires self-compassion, self-acceptance, and a supportive environment. Teenagers have the capacity to navigate media influence, build self-esteem, adopt healthy habits, and create a positive atmosphere that celebrates individuality and diversity.

Remember that your worth is not determined by your appearance, and you are unique and valuable just as you are. Embrace your individuality, prioritize self-care, and surround yourself with people who lift you up and appreciate you for who you are. By taking these steps, teenagers can cultivate a positive body image and a strong sense of self-worth that will serve them well throughout their lives.

Promoting a healthy body image is essential for mental and physical well-being.

Chapter 7: Peer Pressure and Its Impact

Peer pressure is a ubiquitous aspect of teenage life, and it can have a profound impact on decision-making and behaviour. In this chapter, we will explore the sources of peer pressure, strategies for resisting negative influences, and success stories from teenagers around the world who have navigated the challenges of peer pressure.

Sources of Peer Pressure

Understanding the Origins of Influence

Peer pressure can come from various sources, and recognizing them is the first step in addressing its impact. We will discuss:

- Social Influences: How your social circle can shape your choices and behaviours.
- Media and Advertising: The role of media and marketing in promoting certain behaviours and lifestyles.
- Societal Expectations: The pressures to conform to societal norms and expectations.
- Online Influences: How online communities and trends can impact your decisions.

Understanding where peer pressure originates can empower you to make informed choices.

Resisting Negative Influences

Empowering You to Say No

Resisting peer pressure can be challenging, but it is possible with the right strategies. We will explore:

- Assertiveness and Communication: Techniques for expressing your boundaries and making your decisions known.
- Peer Support: The importance of surrounding yourself with friends who respect your choices.
- Decision-Making Skills: Strategies for making thoughtful and informed decisions.
- Stress Management: How to cope with the anxiety and stress that can accompany resisting peer pressure.

Empowering Teenagers: Strategies to Navigate Peer Pressure and Make Informed Choices

Teenagers often face significant peer pressure, whether it is related to academics, relationships, substance use, or other aspects of their lives. Learning how to assert themselves, communicate effectively, and make informed decisions is crucial for maintaining their autonomy and well-being. In this comprehensive guide, we will explore techniques for teenagers to deal with assertiveness and communication, seek peer support, develop decision-making skills, and manage the stress associated with resisting peer pressure.

I. Assertiveness and Communication: Expressing Your Boundaries

Assertiveness and effective communication are essential skills for teenagers to navigate peer pressure while staying true to themselves:

A. Understanding Assertiveness
   1. What Is Assertiveness: Recognize that assertiveness is the ability to express your thoughts, feelings, and boundaries respectfully and confidently.
   2. Passive vs. Aggressive vs. Assertive: Understand the differences between passive (not expressing your needs), aggressive (forcing your views on others), and assertive communication styles.

B. Techniques for Assertive Communication
   1. Use "I" Statements: Express your feelings and needs using "I" statements, such as "I feel uncomfortable when..."
   2. Practice Active Listening: Listen actively to others and show empathy by reflecting their feelings and thoughts.

3. Set Clear Boundaries: Clearly define your boundaries and limits to ensure your comfort and well-being.
4. Learn to Say "No": Practice saying "no" when necessary, and provide brief, respectful explanations if needed.

II. Peer Support: The Importance of Respecting Choices

Surrounding oneself with friends who respect one's choices is crucial for resisting peer pressure and maintaining a strong sense of self:

A. Identifying Supportive Friends
   1. Qualities of Supportive Friends: Recognize the qualities of supportive friends, such as empathy, respect, and the ability to listen without judgment.
   2. Open and Honest Communication: Foster open and honest communication with friends to build trust.
   3. Peer Pressure vs. Peer Support: Differentiate between peer pressure (negative influence) and peer support (positive influence).

B. Handling Peer Pressure
   1. Resist Negative Influence: Develop the confidence to resist negative peer pressure by maintaining your values and boundaries.
   2. Peer Pressure Scripts: Practice assertive responses to common peer pressure situations, such as declining drugs or alcohol.

3. Peer Supportive Responses: Encourage friends to support your choices and say no to peer pressure together.

III. Decision-Making Skills: Making Thoughtful Choices

Effective decision-making skills empower teenagers to make informed and thoughtful choices in the face of peer pressure:

A. The Decision-Making Process
   1. Identify the Decision: Clearly define the decision you need to make, such as whether to attend a party or engage in a certain activity.
   2. Gather Information: Collect relevant information about the options and potential consequences.
   3. Consider Values and Goals: Reflect on your values, goals, and priorities to align your decision with your beliefs.
   4. Evaluate Risks and Benefits: Weigh the risks and benefits of each option to make an informed choice.

B. Strategies for Informed Decisions
   1. Pros and Cons List: Create a list of pros and cons for each option to visualize the potential outcomes.
   2. Consult Trusted Adults: Seek guidance and advice from trusted adults, such as parents, teachers, or mentors.

3. Use Critical Thinking: Apply critical thinking skills to analyse information objectively and make rational decisions.
4. Trust Your Instincts: Trust your intuition and gut feelings when making decisions.

IV. Stress Management: Coping with the Anxiety of Resisting Peer Pressure

Resisting peer pressure can be stressful and anxiety-inducing. Learning how to manage stress is crucial for maintaining mental and emotional well-being:

A. Recognizing Stress
   1. Physical and Emotional Signs: Identify physical and emotional signs of stress, such as increased heart rate, tension, or irritability.
   2. Triggers: Recognize situations or thoughts that trigger stress related to peer pressure.
B. Stress Management Techniques
   1. Deep Breathing: Practice deep breathing exercises to calm your body and reduce anxiety.
   2. Mindfulness and Meditation: Use mindfulness and meditation techniques to stay present and alleviate stress.
   3. Positive Self-Talk: Challenge negative self-talk and replace it with positive affirmations.

4. Seek Support: Reach out to friends, family, or professionals when you are feeling overwhelmed.
5. Time Management: Manage your time effectively to reduce the pressure of deadlines and obligations.

Teenagers face peer pressure in various aspects of their lives, but with the right skills and strategies, they can resist negative influences, make informed choices, and maintain their self-esteem and individuality. Assertiveness and effective communication enable them to express their boundaries, while supportive friends provide a foundation of respect and understanding. Decision-making skills empower teenagers to weigh their options and align their choices with their values and goals. Additionally, stress management techniques help them cope with the anxiety that may accompany resisting peer pressure.

Remember that peer pressure is a part of adolescence, but it does not have to dictate your choices. By developing these skills and seeking support when needed, teenagers can navigate peer pressure with confidence and integrity, ultimately shaping their own paths and futures.

Empower yourself to make choices that align with your values and aspirations.

By the end of this section, you will have a comprehensive understanding of confronting bullying, recognizing eating disorders and promoting a healthy body image, and navigating the challenges of peer pressure. These topics are crucial elements of interpersonal relationships, and the insights and strategies provided will empower you to foster healthy relationships, make informed decisions, and prioritize your well-being in your teenage journey.

CHAPTER 8: Mastering Money Management

Effective money management is a crucial skill that can greatly impact your future financial well-being. In this chapter, we will explore budgeting and saving tips, discuss financial responsibility for teens.

Budgeting and Saving Tips

Building a Strong Financial Foundation

Managing money begins with budgeting and saving. We will provide you with practical tips on:

- Creating a Budget: How to outline your income and expenses, and allocate funds wisely.
- Setting Financial Goals: The importance of setting achievable financial goals and tracking your progress.
- Smart Saving Strategies: Ways to save money, build an emergency fund, and plan for future expenses.
- Avoiding Impulse Purchases: Techniques to resist the temptation of unnecessary spending.
- Understanding the Power of Compound Interest: How saving and investing early can lead to financial growth over time.

By mastering budgeting and saving, you can build a strong financial foundation for your future.

Financial Responsibility for Teens

Understanding Financial Basics

To become financially responsible, you need to understand essential financial concepts and practices, such as:

- Banking Basics: How to open and manage a bank account, and the importance of maintaining a positive banking history.
- Credit and Debt: The impact of credit scores, responsible credit card use, and managing debt effectively.
- Income and Taxes: Understanding income sources, taxation, and the importance of filing taxes when necessary.
- Financial Independence: Preparing for financial independence as you transition into adulthood.

Financial Literacy for Teenagers: A Comprehensive Guide to Building a Strong Financial Foundation

Financial literacy is a critical life skill that empowers teenagers to make informed decisions about their money and plan for a secure financial future. As teenagers transition into adulthood, they face various financial challenges, from opening and managing a bank account to understanding credit and debt, handling income and taxes, and preparing for financial independence. This comprehensive guide aims to equip teenagers with the knowledge and skills needed to navigate these financial aspects successfully.

I. Banking Basics: Opening and Managing a Bank Account

Understanding the fundamentals of banking is essential for teenagers as they begin to manage their money independently:

A. Importance of a Bank Account

   1. Secure Place for Money: A bank account provides a safe place to store and manage money, reducing the risk of loss or theft.
   2. Convenient Payment Method: Bank accounts enable electronic transactions, making it easier to pay bills and make purchases.
   3. Building Financial History: Establishing a positive banking history can be crucial for future financial opportunities, such as loans or mortgages.

B. How to Open a Bank Account

   1. Choose the Right Bank: Research different banks and their account types to find one that suits your needs and offers low or no fees.
   2. Gather Required Documents: Prepare the necessary identification and documentation, such as a driver's license or passport.

3. Visit the Bank: Schedule an appointment with the bank, and a representative will guide you through the account-opening process.

C. Managing a Bank Account

1. Monitoring Balances: Regularly check your account balance to ensure you have enough funds to cover expenses and avoid overdraft fees.
2. Tracking Transactions: Keep track of all transactions, including deposits and withdrawals, to maintain an accurate record of your finances.
3. Online and Mobile Banking: Utilize online and mobile banking services for convenience and easy access to your account.
4. Savings Account: Consider opening a savings account to start building an emergency fund or saving for future goals.

II. Credit and Debt: Building a Positive Credit History

Understanding credit and debt is crucial for teenagers as they start to use credit cards and loans responsibly:

A. Credit Scores and Their Importance

1. What Is a Credit Score: Learn what a credit score is and how it is calculated based on your credit history.
2. Importance of a Good Credit Score: Understand that a good credit score can lead to lower interest rates on loans and better financial opportunities.

OWL STRETCHING AND OTHER ISSUES...

- B. Responsible Credit Card Use
    1. Choosing a Credit Card: Research different credit cards and select one with reasonable terms, low fees, and a manageable credit limit.
    2. Credit Card Usage Tips: Learn how to use a credit card responsibly by paying bills on time, avoiding carrying a high balance, and using it for essential expenses.
    3. Building Credit: Use a credit card to build a positive credit history by making timely payments and keeping your credit utilization low.
- C. Managing Debt Effectively
    1. Avoiding Excessive Debt: Understand the dangers of accumulating excessive debt, such as high-interest loans and credit card debt.
    2. Creating a Repayment Plan: If you have debt, develop a repayment plan that prioritizes paying off high-interest debt first.
    3. Seeking Help When Needed: Reach out to a credit counsellor or financial advisor if you struggle with managing debt or need guidance on repayment strategies.

III. Income and Taxes: Understanding Your Finances

As teenagers begin earning income, they should grasp the basics of income sources and taxation:

A. Sources of Income
    1. Earned Income: Understand that earned income comes from employment, such as part-time jobs or internships.
    2. Passive Income: Learn about passive income, which can be generated from investments, rental properties, or business ventures.
B. Taxes and Their Importance
    1. What Are Taxes: Gain a basic understanding of taxes as mandatory financial contributions to the government.
    2. Types of Taxes: Learn about various types of taxes, including income tax, sales tax, and property tax.
    3. Filing Taxes: Know when and how to file taxes, and understand the consequences of failing to do so.
C. Budgeting and Financial Planning
    1. Budgeting Basics: Develop a budget to manage your income effectively, allocate funds for essential expenses, savings, and discretionary spending.
    2. Emergency Fund: Prioritize building an emergency fund to cover unexpected expenses and financial emergencies.

IV. Financial Independence: Preparing for Adulthood

As teenagers transition into adulthood, they should prepare for financial independence and responsible money management:

A. Financial Goal Setting
   1. Short-Term and Long-Term Goals: Set both short-term goals, such as saving for a new gadget, and long-term goals, like planning for higher education or homeownership.
   2. SMART Goals: Apply the SMART criteria (Specific, Measurable, Achievable, Relevant, Time-bound) to your financial goals.

B. Higher Education and Career Planning
   1. Exploring Career Options: Research and explore potential career paths to align your education and training with your interests and goals.
   2. Financial Aid and Scholarships: Investigate opportunities for financial aid and scholarships to support your education and reduce student loan debt.

C. Savings and Investment Strategies
   1. Investing Basics: Understand the fundamentals of investing and consider strategies to grow your wealth over time.

2. Retirement Planning: Start saving for retirement early, as compound interest can significantly impact your future financial security.

D. Responsible Financial Decision-Making
1. Seeking Professional Advice: When facing complex financial decisions, consider consulting with a financial advisor or counsellor for expert guidance.
2. Avoiding Impulse Spending: Be mindful of impulsive spending and make thoughtful financial choices.

Financial literacy is a vital skill that empowers teenagers to make informed financial decisions, manage their money responsibly, and plan for a secure future. By understanding banking basics, credit and debt management, income, and taxes, and preparing for financial independence, teenagers can develop a strong financial foundation that will serve them well throughout their lives. Remember that financial education is an ongoing process, and with continuous learning and responsible financial practices, teenagers can build a solid financial future.

Taking responsibility for your finances is a critical step toward achieving long-term financial success.

Part III

Personal Development

In this section, we will explore personal development topics that are crucial for your growth during your teenage years. We will discuss strategies for cultivating motivation and ambition, navigating substance use, and provide testimonies of recovery.

Chapter 9: Cultivating Motivation and Ambition

Motivation and ambition are the driving forces behind personal growth and achievement. In this chapter, we will explore strategies for boosting motivation, setting and achieving goals, and share inspiring stories of teenagers who have achieved greatness.

Strategies for Boosting Motivation

Staying Driven and Inspired

Maintaining motivation can be challenging, but there are effective strategies to help you stay driven, including:

- Setting Clear Goals: How to define your goals and break them down into manageable steps.
- Finding Purpose: Discovering your passions and aligning them with your goals.
- Creating a Vision Board: A visual representation of your goals and aspirations.
- Accountability Partners: The benefits of sharing your goals with others who can hold you accountable.
- Overcoming Procrastination: Techniques for combating procrastination and staying on track.

Achieving Goals

Turning Dreams into Reality

Setting goals is just the first step; achieving them is the ultimate objective. We will explore:

- Goal-Setting Strategies: Effective methods for setting SMART (Specific, Measurable, Achievable, Relevant, Time-bound) goals.
- Creating Action Plans: Outlining the steps needed to reach your goals and tracking your progress.
- Perseverance and Resilience: Strategies for overcoming setbacks and staying committed to your goals.
- Celebrating Successes: The importance of recognizing and celebrating your achievements along the way.

A Teenager's Guide to Achieving Success: Goal Setting, Action Planning, Perseverance, and Celebration

As teenagers embark on their journey toward adulthood, setting and achieving goals becomes a crucial part of their personal growth and development. The ability to set meaningful goals, create effective action plans, persevere in the face of challenges, and celebrate successes is a fundamental life skill. In this comprehensive guide, we will explore strategies that teenagers can use to set SMART goals, create action plans, develop perseverance and resilience, and celebrate their achievements along the way.

I. Goal-Setting Strategies: The Power of SMART Goals

Setting goals that are Specific, Measurable, Achievable, Relevant, and Time-bound (SMART) is a proven method for success:

A. Specific Goals
    1. Clarity: Define your goals with precision, leaving no room for ambiguity.
    2. Examples: Instead of a vague goal like "get better at school," set a specific goal like "improve my math grade from a C to a B."
B. Measurable Goals
    1. Quantify Your Goals: Make your goals measurable by assigning numbers, percentages, or other quantifiable criteria.
    2. Track Progress: Use metrics to track your progress and determine if you're on the right path.
C. Achievable Goals
    1. Realistic Assessments: Ensure your goals are achievable by realistically evaluating your current resources and abilities.
    2. Set Milestones: Break down larger goals into smaller, attainable milestones.

D. Relevant Goals
   1. Alignment with Values: Ensure your goals align with your personal values and aspirations.
   2. Prioritization: Focus on goals that are relevant to your current life stage and long-term objectives.
E. Time-Bound Goals
   1. Set Deadlines: Establish specific deadlines for your goals to create a sense of urgency.
   2. Avoid Procrastination: Time-bound goals help prevent procrastination and keep you accountable.

II. Creating Action Plans: The Roadmap to Achievement

Once you've set SMART goals, it's essential to create action plans that outline the steps needed to reach those goals:

A. Define Specific Actions
   1. Break It Down: List the specific actions or tasks required to achieve your goal.
   2. Sequence Matters: Organize these actions in a logical sequence.
B. Set Timelines
   1. Deadline for Each Action: Assign deadlines to each action to create a timeline for your plan.
   2. Prioritize Tasks: Prioritize tasks based on their importance and urgency.

C. Allocate Resources

   1. Identify Resources: Determine the resources, tools, and support needed for each action.
   2. Budget Wisely: If necessary, allocate a budget for expenses related to your goals.

D. Monitor and Adjust

   1. Regularly Review: Keep track of your progress by reviewing your action plan frequently.
   2. Adapt and Adjust: Be willing to adjust your plan if you encounter obstacles or if circumstances change.

III. Perseverance and Resilience: Overcoming Setbacks

Setbacks are a natural part of pursuing goals. Developing perseverance and resilience is essential for overcoming obstacles:

A. Maintain a Growth Mindset

   1. Embrace Challenges: View challenges as opportunities for growth rather than insurmountable obstacles.
   2. Learn from Failure: Extract valuable lessons from failures and use them to improve.

B. Stay Committed

   1. Focus on Your Why: Remind yourself why your goal is important to stay motivated.

2. Small Steps: If progress slows, break tasks into smaller, manageable steps to maintain momentum.

C. Seek Support
   1. Lean on Others: Reach out to friends, family, mentors, or support groups for encouragement and guidance.
   2. Ask for Help: Don't hesitate to ask for help or advice when facing difficulties.

D. Self-Care
   1. Prioritize Well-being: Take care of your physical and mental health to maintain the energy and resilience needed for goal pursuit.
   2. Balance: Balance your efforts by setting aside time for relaxation and rejuvenation.

IV. Celebrating Successes: The Importance of Acknowledgment

Celebrating achievements, no matter how small, is a critical part of staying motivated and maintaining a positive outlook:

A. Acknowledge Milestones
   1. Small Wins: Celebrate small achievements and milestones along the way.
   2. Positive Reinforcement: Acknowledge your progress to reinforce positive behaviours.

B. Reflect on Achievements
   1. Journaling: Maintain a journal to record your accomplishments and reflect on your journey.
   2. Gratitude: Practice gratitude by acknowledging the people and circumstances that supported your success.
C. Share Your Success
   1. Inspire Others: Share your achievements with friends and family to inspire and motivate others.
   2. Feedback Loop: Use positive feedback from others to reinforce your sense of accomplishment.

The ability to set SMART goals, create effective action plans, develop perseverance and resilience, and celebrate successes is a powerful combination for achieving personal and academic goals. As teenagers transition into adulthood, these skills will serve as a foundation for success in various aspects of life. Remember that goal setting is not only about reaching the destination but also about embracing the journey and the growth it brings. With determination, resilience, and the strategies outlined in this guide, teenagers can set and achieve meaningful goals that contribute to their personal development and future success.

Chapter 10: Navigating Substance Use

Substance use is a prevalent issue among teenagers, and it's essential to understand the risks, make informed choices, and seek help if needed. In this chapter, we will explore the issues related to drug and alcohol use, strategies for making informed choices, and share testimonies of recovery.

Understanding Drug and Alcohol Issues

Awareness and Education

Understanding the issues related to drug and alcohol use is the first step in making informed decisions. We'll discuss:

- Types of Substances: An overview of common drugs and alcohol, their effects, and associated risks.
- Peer Pressure and Influence: How peer pressure can play a role in substance use decisions.
- The Impact on Health and Well-being: The physical, mental, and social consequences of substance use.
- Recognizing a Problem: How to identify signs of substance abuse and addiction.

Making Informed Choices

Empowering You to Choose Wisely

Making informed choices about substance use is crucial for your health and well-being. We'll explore:

- Drug and Alcohol Education: The importance of understanding the risks associated with substance use.
- Responsible Decision-Making: Strategies for saying no to substances and resisting peer pressure.
- Seeking Help: How to seek support and assistance if you or someone you know is struggling with substance abuse.

Empowering Teenagers: A Comprehensive Guide to Drug and Alcohol Education, Responsible Decision-Making, and Seeking Help

As teenagers navigate the complexities of adolescence, they often encounter situations involving drugs and alcohol. Understanding the risks associated with substance use, making responsible decisions, and knowing how to seek help are essential life skills that can protect their well-being. In this comprehensive guide, we will explore the importance of drug and alcohol education, strategies for responsible decision-making, and how to seek support and assistance if teenagers or someone they know is struggling with substance abuse.

I. Drug and Alcohol Education: Understanding the Risks

A solid foundation in drug and alcohol education is the first step in making informed decisions:

A. Understanding Substance Categories
    1. Legal and Illegal Substances: Differentiate between legal substances (e.g., alcohol, nicotine) and illegal substances (e.g., marijuana, cocaine).
    2. Types of Drugs: Learn about various drug categories, including depressants, stimulants, hallucinogens, and opioids.
B. The Risks of Substance Abuse
    1. Physical Health Risks: Understand the physical consequences of substance abuse, such as addiction, overdose, and long-term health issues.
    2. Mental Health Impact: Recognize how substance abuse can contribute to mental health problems, including anxiety, depression, and psychosis.
    3. Social and Legal Consequences: Explore the potential social and legal ramifications of drug and alcohol use, including impaired judgment and legal trouble.
C. Recognizing Peer Pressure
    1. Peer Influence: Understand the role of peer pressure in substance use and how it can impact decision-making.

2. Resisting Peer Pressure: Learn strategies for confidently saying no to substances and resisting peer pressure.

II. Responsible Decision-Making: Strategies for Saying No

Making responsible decisions about drug and alcohol use requires a combination of awareness and effective strategies:

A. Self-Reflection
   1. Clarify Your Values: Identify your personal values and boundaries related to substance use.
   2. Future Goals: Consider how substance use may impact your long-term goals and aspirations.

B. Strategies for Saying No
   1. Assertive Communication: Practice assertive responses when declining substances, using "I" statements, and expressing your reasons clearly.
   2. Plan Ahead: Prepare responses in advance for situations where you may face peer pressure.
   3. Exit Strategies: Develop exit strategies to remove yourself from situations involving substances.
   4. Use of Alternatives: Suggest alternative activities or gatherings that do not involve substance use.

C. Understanding Consequences

   1. Short-Term vs. Long-Term Consequences: Evaluate the potential short-term gratification versus the long-term consequences of substance use.
   2. Personal Responsibility: Emphasize the importance of taking responsibility for your actions and choices.

III. Seeking Help: Support and Assistance

Recognizing when to seek help for substance abuse, whether for oneself or a friend, is a crucial skill:

A. Signs of Substance Abuse

   1. Behavioural Changes: Be aware of behavioural signs, such as increased secrecy, mood swings, or declining academic performance.
   2. Physical Symptoms: Recognize physical signs, such as bloodshot eyes, dilated pupils, or unusual odours on the breath.
   3. Social Withdrawal: Pay attention to changes in social relationships, including isolation from friends and family.

B. Seeking Support for Yourself

   1. Confide in Trusted Individuals: Reach out to a trusted friend, family member, or mentor if you are struggling with substance abuse.

2. Professional Help: Understand the role of therapists, counsellors, and substance abuse treatment programs in recovery.
3. Support Groups: Explore the benefits of joining support groups for individuals facing similar challenges.

C. Supporting a Friend in Need

1. Open and Non-Judgmental Communication: Approach your friend with empathy, understanding, and an open dialogue.
2. Encourage Professional Help: Suggest seeking help from professionals or support groups.
3. Respect Boundaries: Respect your friend's boundaries and choices, even if they are not ready for help.

D. Emergency Situations

1. Recognize Overdose: Learn the signs of an overdose and the importance of seeking immediate medical assistance.
2. Emergency Contacts: Keep emergency contacts readily accessible and call 911 if necessary.

IV. Treatment and Recovery

Understanding the stages of treatment and recovery is essential for those dealing with substance abuse issues:

A. Assessment and Evaluation

   1. Professional Assessment: Recognize the importance of professional assessments to determine the extent of substance abuse.
   2. Treatment Options: Explore different treatment options, such as outpatient therapy, inpatient programs, or medication-assisted treatment.

B. Rehabilitation and Recovery

   1. Detoxification: Understand the role of detox programs in managing withdrawal symptoms.
   2. Therapy and Counselling: Learn about the benefits of individual and group therapy in addressing the root causes of substance abuse.
   3. Relapse Prevention: Explore strategies and skills for preventing relapse and maintaining sobriety.

C. Support Systems

   1. Supportive Network: Build a network of friends, family, and support groups to provide ongoing encouragement.
   2. Long-Term Recovery: Understand that recovery is a lifelong journey, and ongoing support is crucial.

Drug and alcohol education, responsible decision-making, and knowing how to seek help are essential life skills that empower teenagers to make informed choices regarding substance use. By understanding the risks associated with substance abuse, developing strategies for saying no to peer pressure, and knowing how to seek support and assistance when needed, teenagers can protect their well-being and make responsible decisions that align with their values and goals. Remember that seeking help is a sign of strength, and recovery is possible with the right resources and support.

By the end of this section, you will have a comprehensive understanding of mastering money management, cultivating motivation and ambition, and navigating substance use. These topics are essential for your personal development and well-being during your teenage years, and the insights, strategies, and real-life stories provided will empower you to make informed decisions, set and achieve meaningful goals, and build a brighter future.

CHAPTER 11: Interacting with Law Enforcement

Interacting with law enforcement is a significant aspect of teenage life, and it's essential to understand your rights and responsibilities, aim for positive encounters, and know where to find legal resources when needed.

Rights and Responsibilities

Knowing Your Role in Legal Interactions

Understanding your rights and responsibilities when interacting with law enforcement is crucial. We'll discuss:

- Your Legal Rights: An overview of rights,
- Interacting with Police: Tips for staying calm and respectful during encounters with law enforcement.
- Traffic Stops and Searches: What to do when pulled over by the police and understanding search procedures.
- Juvenile Justice: How the legal system treats teenagers, including the importance of understanding the consequences of your actions.

Teenagers' Guide to Understanding Legal Rights and Interactions with Law Enforcement in the United Kingdom

As teenagers in the United Kingdom transition into adulthood, it's essential to understand their legal rights and responsibilities, as well as how to navigate interactions with law enforcement. This comprehensive guide will provide valuable insights into your legal rights, tips for interacting with the police, what to do during traffic stops and searches, and the workings of the juvenile justice system. By gaining this knowledge, teenagers can confidently assert their rights while staying respectful and informed within the bounds of the law.

I. Your Legal Rights: An Overview

A. The Right to Legal Counsel
    1. Representation: Understand your right to legal representation when facing criminal charges or being questioned by the police.
    2. Duty Solicitor: Learn about the role of the duty solicitor, who provides free legal advice when in custody.

B. The Right to Remain Silent
    1. The Right to Silence: Recognize your right to remain silent and avoid self-incrimination when questioned by the police.

2. Voluntary Statements: Understand that any statements you make to the police must be voluntary.

C. The Right to Privacy

1. Protection from Unlawful Searches: Learn about your protection from unreasonable and invasive searches of your property and person.
2. Data Protection: Understand your rights concerning the collection and use of your personal data.

D. The Right to a Fair Trial

1. Presumption of Innocence: Embrace the presumption of innocence until proven guilty in a court of law.
2. Trial by Jury: Understand the right to a trial by jury for serious criminal offenses.

II. Interacting with Police: Tips for Staying Calm and Respectful

A. Staying Calm and Composed

1. Remain Calm: Keep your composure and remain respectful when interacting with law enforcement.
2. Avoid Confrontation: Understand the importance of avoiding confrontational behaviour or language.

OWL STRETCHING AND OTHER ISSUES...

B. Asserting Your Rights Respectfully

   1. Politely Request Clarification: Politely ask for clarification if you are unsure about your rights during an encounter with the police.
   2. Respectful Tone: Maintain a respectful tone and demeanour when asserting your rights.

C. Record the Encounter

   1. Right to Record: Know that you have the right to record interactions with the police, provided you do so safely and without obstructing their duties.
   2. Notifying the Officer: Inform the officer that you are recording, if possible.

III. Traffic Stops and Searches: Understanding Procedures

A. Traffic Stops

   1. Pulled Over by the Police: Know what to do when pulled over by the police, such as pulling over safely and turning off your engine.
   2. Providing Documents: Understand the requirement to provide your driving license, insurance, and vehicle registration.

B. Searches

   1. Searches with Consent: Learn about searches that require your consent and your right to refuse.

2. Stop and Search: Understand the "stop and search" powers of the police and the importance of cooperation.

In the United Kingdom, like in many other countries, individuals have rights when it comes to searches by law enforcement or other authorities. It's essential to understand your rights and when you can give or refuse consent for a search. Here's some advice on searches with consent in the UK:

Know Your Rights: It's crucial to be aware of your rights. In the UK, police officers or other authorities must have reasonable grounds to stop and search you or your property without consent. These grounds might include suspicion of carrying illegal drugs, weapons, or evidence of a crime. If you are stopped, you have the right to ask the officer for their name, rank, and the station they are from.

Consensual Searches: In some cases, the police or authorities may ask for your consent to conduct a search. You have the right to refuse this request. You are under no obligation to give consent if there are no reasonable grounds for the search. You can simply say, "I do not consent to a search."

Remaining Calm and Polite: If you are approached by the police, it's essential to remain calm and polite. You have the right to ask questions, but it's generally best to comply with lawful requests and challenge them later, if necessary.

Recording the Encounter: You have the right to record encounters with the police or other authorities using your smartphone or other recording devices, as long as it doesn't obstruct their work. This can be helpful if you believe your rights are being violated, but it's important to do so without interfering with the search.

Legal Representation: If you believe that your rights have been violated during a search, you should seek legal advice. Your solicitor can guide you on whether there is a case for unlawful search and potential actions to take.

Stay Informed: Laws and regulations may change, so it's essential to stay informed about your rights. This information is available on government websites, and advocacy organizations can also provide guidance.

Community and Legal Support: In some cases, it may be helpful to reach out to community organizations or legal advocacy groups for support and advice if you encounter repeated issues with searches and feel that your rights are not being respected.

Cooperate When Necessary: While you have the right to refuse consent to a search, it's also important to understand when cooperation is in your best interest. For example, if you have been stopped on reasonable grounds and the police have a warrant, resisting may not be wise. In such cases, consult with a legal representative after the fact.

Remember that the information provided here is general advice and should not be considered as legal advice specific to your situation. If you ever have concerns about searches, it's a good idea to consult with a solicitor or legal expert who can provide guidance tailored to your circumstances.

IV. Juvenile Justice: Understanding the Consequences

A. Legal Responsibilities as a Teenager
    1. Age of Criminal Responsibility: Know the age at which you can be held criminally responsible for your actions.
    2. The age of criminal responsibility in the United Kingdom is 10 years old. This means that children aged 10 and above can be held criminally responsible for their actions and may be subject to criminal charges and court proceedings if they are found to have committed a criminal offense.

        It's important to note that children under the age of 10 are considered legally incapable of committing a crime in the UK. Instead, their actions are typically addressed through child welfare and social services, focusing on their well-being and rehabilitation rather than criminal punishment.

However, the criminal justice system for children and young people in the UK is distinct from the adult system and emphasizes rehabilitation, support, and education. Special provisions and protections are in place to safeguard the rights and best interests of children who come into contact with the criminal justice system.

It's also worth mentioning that the age of criminal responsibility can vary from one country to another, and it's subject to legal and cultural differences. In the UK, there have been discussions and debates about whether the age of criminal responsibility should be raised to ensure better protection of young children's rights and well-being, but as of my last knowledge update in September 2021, the age remains at 10.

3. Consequences of Offenses: Understand the potential legal consequences, including fines, community service, or custody.

B. Rehabilitation and Support

1. Youth Offender Teams: Learn about Youth Offender Teams that provide support, rehabilitation, and supervision for young offenders.

2. Youth Rehabilitation Orders: Understand the conditions and requirements of Youth Rehabilitation Orders.

C. Avoiding Criminal Records

1. Cautions and Warnings: Recognize the implications of receiving cautions or warnings and their impact on your record.

   In the United Kingdom, receiving cautions and warnings from law enforcement can have various implications, particularly in the context of a person's criminal record and future prospects. Here are the key impacts of cautions and warnings in the UK:

   No Criminal Conviction: Both cautions and warnings are typically used for less serious offenses and do not result in a criminal conviction. They are considered an alternative to prosecution and are intended to divert individuals away from the criminal justice system.

   Record of the Offense: While cautions and warnings do not lead to a criminal conviction, they are recorded on your police record. This means that law enforcement agencies will have a record of the caution or warning you received.

   Disclosure to Employers: Depending on the type of caution or warning and the context, you may be required to disclose this information to potential employers. Some employers, especially those working with vulnerable populations or in certain regulated sectors, may ask about any prior cautions or warnings.

DBS Checks: The Disclosure and Barring Service (DBS) checks, previously known as CRB checks, are used in various industries, such as education, healthcare, and social work, to assess an individual's background. Depending on the nature of the caution or warning, it may or may not appear on a DBS check. In some cases, cautions and warnings are filtered out and do not need to be disclosed on standard or enhanced checks.

Impact on Future Employment: While minor cautions and warnings may not severely impact your employment prospects, more serious or multiple cautions and warnings may raise concerns with some employers. It's important to be honest and transparent when asked about your criminal history.

Education and Licensing: Certain educational institutions and professional licensing bodies may inquire about cautions and warnings when assessing applications. The impact on your education and career can vary depending on the specifics of the offense and the institution or body's policies.

Rehabilitation Periods: In some cases, cautions and warnings become "spent" after a certain period. This means that they no longer need to be disclosed in many situations. The length of the rehabilitation period depends on the type of caution or warning.

Legal Advice: If you have concerns about the implications of a caution or warning on your record, it's advisable to seek legal advice. A solicitor can provide guidance on your specific situation and advise you on the best course of action.

It's important to remember that cautions and warnings are generally designed to offer individuals a second chance and divert them from more serious consequences. However, they should not be taken lightly, and individuals should be aware of the potential long-term implications, especially in situations where disclosure is required. Additionally, laws and regulations can change, so it's wise to stay informed about the most current guidelines regarding cautions and warnings in the UK.

2. Spent Convictions: Understand the concept of spent convictions and how they may affect future opportunities.

As teenagers in the United Kingdom, it is vital to be aware of your legal rights, interact respectfully with law enforcement, understand the procedures during traffic stops and searches, and grasp the workings of the juvenile justice system. Knowledge of your rights and responsibilities empowers you to navigate legal situations confidently and responsibly. Remember that staying informed and respectful is key to maintaining a positive relationship with law enforcement and ensuring that your rights are protected throughout any interactions with the criminal justice system.

Positive Encounters with Police

Building Trust and Cooperation

Positive interactions with law enforcement can foster trust and cooperation. We'll explore:

- Communication Skills: Techniques for effective and respectful communication with police officers.
- De-escalation Strategies: How to maintain a calm demeanour during stressful encounters.
- Knowing When to Seek Legal Counsel: When and how to involve an attorney in legal matters.

- Community Policing: Understanding the role of police officers in your community and the importance of community engagement.

A Guide for Teenagers in the United Kingdom: Effective Communication, De-escalation, Legal Counsel, and Community Policing

Navigating interactions with law enforcement can be a complex and daunting task, especially for teenagers in the United Kingdom. This comprehensive guide aims to equip teenagers with essential knowledge and skills related to communication, de-escalation, seeking legal counsel, and understanding the role of community policing. By developing these skills and understanding the context of law enforcement in their communities, teenagers can approach such encounters with confidence and respect for their rights.

I. Communication Skills: Techniques for Effective and Respectful Communication

A. Active Listening
  1. Pay Attention: Focus on the officer's words and non-verbal cues to demonstrate active listening.
  2. Ask Clarifying Questions: Seek clarification if you do not understand the officer's instructions or questions.

B. Clear and Respectful Language
   1. Use Polite Language: Address officers respectfully by using "sir" or "ma'am."
   2. Avoid Arguments: Refrain from engaging in arguments or confrontational language.
C. Stay Calm and Composed
   1. Control Emotions: Practice emotional self-regulation to maintain a calm demeanour.
   2. Breathe Deeply: Use deep breathing techniques to reduce stress and anxiety.

II. De-escalation Strategies: Maintaining a Calm Demeanour

A. Non-Threatening Body Language
   1. Open Posture: Maintain an open and non-threatening posture to convey cooperation.
   2. Avoid Sudden Movements: Make slow and deliberate movements to avoid alarming the officer.
B. Verbal De-escalation
   1. Stay Respectful: Maintain a respectful tone and language, even in tense situations.
   2. Empathize and Listen: Show empathy by acknowledging the officer's perspective and actively listening.

C. Compliance

   1. Follow Instructions: Comply with lawful instructions from the police to reduce tension.
   2. Assert Rights Respectfully: Politely assert your rights, when necessary, without confrontation.

III. Knowing When to Seek Legal Counsel

A. Arrest and Detention

   1. The Right to Legal Counsel: Understand your right to consult with an attorney when arrested or detained.
   2. Access to Duty Solicitor: Know that you have access to a duty solicitor while in custody.

B. Questioning by Police

   1. Remaining Silent: Exercise your right to remain silent when questioned by the police.
   2. Requesting an Attorney: Politely request an attorney before answering any questions if you believe it is necessary.

C. Legal Representation

   1. Private Solicitor: Learn about the option to hire a private solicitor to represent your interests.
   2. Legal Aid: Explore the availability of legal aid for those who cannot afford private representation.

IV. Community Policing: Understanding the Role of Police in Your Community

A. Community Engagement

    1. Building Positive Relationships: Recognize the importance of community-police partnerships in enhancing public safety.
    2. Community Policing Initiatives: Participate in community programs and initiatives aimed at fostering positive interactions with law enforcement.

B. Police Accountability

    1. Know Your Rights: Familiarize yourself with your rights and how they are protected by law.
    2. Reporting Misconduct: Understand the process for reporting police misconduct or abuse.

C. Bridging Gaps

    1. Dialogue and Communication: Promote open dialogue between community members and law enforcement to address concerns and build trust.
    2. Understanding Perspective: Appreciate the perspectives and challenges faced by police officers in your community.

Effective communication, de-escalation, knowing when to seek legal counsel, and understanding the role of community policing are essential skills and knowledge for teenagers in the United Kingdom. These abilities enable teenagers to engage respectfully with law enforcement, maintain their rights, and actively participate in building safer and more harmonious communities. By approaching law enforcement encounters with confidence and awareness, teenagers can help foster positive relationships between the police and the community, ultimately contributing to a more just and secure society.

Legal Resources for Teens

Accessing Support and Guidance

Knowing where to find legal resources is essential. Search online for...

- Youth Advocacy Organizations: Organizations that provide support and advocacy for young people involved with the legal system.
- Legal Aid: Resources for accessing free or low-cost legal representation when needed.
- Know Your Rights Workshops: The benefits of attending workshops and seminars to learn more about your legal rights.

Empower yourself with knowledge and resources to navigate legal interactions effectively and responsibly.

CHAPTER 12: Building Healthy Relationships

Healthy relationships are the cornerstone of a fulfilling life. In this chapter, we'll explore communication skills, conflict resolution, and learn of the power of positive relationships.

Communication Skills

The Key to Strong Connections

Effective communication is fundamental to building healthy relationships. We'll discuss:

- Active Listening: Techniques for truly hearing and understanding others.
- Assertive Communication: Strategies for expressing your needs and boundaries respectfully.
- Nonverbal Communication: Understanding body language and its role in communication.
- Digital Communication: The impact of technology on modern relationships and how to use it mindfully.

Effective Communication Skills for Teenagers: Active Listening, Assertive Communication, Nonverbal Communication, and Digital Communication

Effective communication is a vital life skill that impacts every aspect of a teenager's personal and social life. From building healthy relationships to succeeding academically, the ability to communicate effectively is essential. In this comprehensive guide, we will explore four crucial facets of communication for teenagers: active listening, assertive communication, nonverbal communication, and digital communication. By mastering these skills, teenagers can enhance their relationships, reduce misunderstandings, and navigate the complexities of the digital age with confidence.

I. Active Listening: Techniques for Truly Hearing and Understanding Others

A. The Art of Active Listening
   1. Definition: Understand what active listening means and why it's essential for effective communication.
   2. Benefits: Recognize the benefits of active listening, such as improved relationships and better problem-solving.

B. Key Techniques

   1. Maintain Eye Contact: Learn how to establish and maintain eye contact to convey attentiveness and interest.
   2. Avoid Interrupting: Practice patience and avoid interrupting when others are speaking.
   3. Reflective Listening: Develop the skill of paraphrasing to confirm your understanding of what the speaker is saying.
   4. Ask Open-Ended Questions: Encourage open communication by asking questions that require more than a simple "yes" or "no" answer.

C. Empathy and Validation

   1. Empathy Defined: Understand the concept of empathy and how it relates to active listening.
   2. Validation: Learn the importance of validating others' feelings and experiences.

II. Assertive Communication: Strategies for Expressing Your Needs and Boundaries Respectfully

A. Assertiveness vs. Passivity and Aggression

   1. Passive Communication: Recognize the characteristics of passive communication, such as avoiding conflict and not expressing one's needs.

2. Aggressive Communication: Identify the traits of aggressive communication, which often involve confrontational and disrespectful behaviour.

B. Assertive Communication Skills

1. Clear and Direct Communication: Practice clear and direct communication to express your needs and boundaries respectfully.
2. I-Statements: Use "I" statements to express feelings and thoughts without blaming or accusing others.
3. Setting Boundaries: Learn how to set and assert healthy boundaries in various relationships.
4. Active Voice: Use the active voice to convey messages more assertively.

C. Handling Criticism and Feedback

1. Receiving Criticism: Discover effective ways to receive criticism without becoming defensive.
2. Providing Feedback: Understand how to provide constructive feedback in a manner that promotes understanding and growth.

III. Nonverbal Communication: Understanding Body Language and Its Role in Communication

A. The Power of Nonverbal Communication

1. Definition: Explore the concept of nonverbal communication, which includes gestures, facial expressions, posture, and tone of voice.

2. Impact: Recognize the significant impact of nonverbal cues on the interpretation of messages.

B. Key Nonverbal Cues

1. Facial Expressions: Understand how facial expressions convey emotions and intentions.
2. Body Language: Learn how posture and body movements can communicate confidence or discomfort.
3. Tone of Voice: Explore how variations in tone can alter the meaning of spoken words.

C. Cross-Cultural Considerations

1. Cultural Differences: Acknowledge that nonverbal cues may be interpreted differently in various cultural contexts.
2. Cultural Sensitivity: Develop cultural sensitivity by seeking to understand and respect others' communication norms.

IV. Digital Communication: The Impact of Technology on Modern Relationships and How to Use It Mindfully

A. The Digital Age

1. Digital Communication Prevalence: Recognize the prevalence of digital communication in everyday life, including texting, social media, and email.

2. Impact on Relationships: Understand how digital communication can influence both positive and negative aspects of relationships.

B. Mindful Digital Communication

1. Digital Etiquette: Practice good digital etiquette by using appropriate language and being respectful online.
2. Avoid Miscommunication: Be aware of the potential for miscommunication in digital messages due to the absence of nonverbal cues.
3. Limit Screen Time: Develop healthy habits for limiting screen time and balancing online and offline interactions.
4. Think Before You Send: Encourage thoughtful and considerate communication by pausing before hitting "send."

Effective communication is a fundamental skill for teenagers, impacting their relationships, personal development, and future success. By mastering active listening, assertive communication, understanding nonverbal cues, and practicing mindful digital communication, teenagers can navigate the challenges of the modern world with confidence and integrity. These skills empower teenagers to express themselves clearly, build positive relationships, and use technology as a tool for meaningful connections rather than a source of misunderstandings and conflict.

Resolving Conflict

Navigating Challenges Together

Conflict is a natural part of any relationship, but it can be resolved constructively. We'll explore:

- Conflict Resolution Strategies: Techniques for addressing and resolving conflicts peacefully.
- Healthy Boundaries: The importance of setting and respecting boundaries in all relationships.
- Forgiveness and Reconciliation: The healing power of forgiveness and rebuilding trust.
- Abusive Relationships: Recognizing signs of abusive relationships and seeking help when necessary.

Building Healthy Relationships: Conflict Resolution, Boundaries, Forgiveness, and Recognizing Abusive Relationships - Advice for Teenagers

Healthy relationships are essential for personal growth and well-being, but they also come with challenges that require effective communication and emotional maturity. This guide provides advice to teenagers on vital aspects of relationships: conflict resolution, setting healthy boundaries, forgiveness, and recognizing and seeking help in abusive relationships. By developing these skills, teenagers can build and maintain positive, respectful, and safe connections with others.

I. Conflict Resolution Strategies: Techniques for Addressing and Resolving Conflicts Peacefully

A. Understanding Conflict

1. Normalizing Conflict: Acknowledge that conflicts are a natural part of relationships and can provide opportunities for growth.
2. Conflict vs. Confrontation: Differentiate between conflict resolution, which seeks a solution, and confrontation, which may escalate tensions.

B. Effective Conflict Resolution Techniques

1. Active Listening: Practice active listening to understand the other person's perspective and feelings.
2. Use "I" Statements: Communicate your feelings and needs using "I" statements to avoid blame.
3. Find Common Ground: Identify shared goals or solutions that satisfy both parties.
4. Stay Calm and Respectful: Manage emotions and maintain a respectful tone during conflicts.

II. Healthy Boundaries: The Importance of Setting and Respecting Boundaries

A. Defining Boundaries

1. What Are Boundaries: Understand that boundaries are personal limits that define acceptable behaviour and interactions.

2. Types of Boundaries: Differentiate between physical, emotional, and social boundaries.

B. Setting Healthy Boundaries

1. Self-Awareness: Reflect on your values, needs, and limits to establish clear boundaries.
2. Communication: Communicate your boundaries assertively and respectfully to others.
3. Consistency: Maintain consistency in enforcing your boundaries to establish trust.

C. Respecting Others' Boundaries

1. Empathy: Understand and respect others' boundaries by putting yourself in their shoes.
2. Consent: Always seek and respect consent in all interactions.

II. Forgiveness and Reconciliation: The Healing Power of Forgiveness and Rebuilding Trust

A. Understanding Forgiveness

1. Forgiveness as a Process: Recognize that forgiveness is a journey and not always immediate.
2. Reconciliation vs. Forgiveness: Differentiate between forgiving someone and choosing to reconcile.

B. The Benefits of Forgiveness

   1. Emotional Healing: Understand how forgiveness can release emotional burdens and promote healing.
   2. Rebuilding Trust: Explore how forgiveness can be a step towards rebuilding trust in relationships.

C. Reconciliation

   1. Mutual Effort: Reconciliation requires effort and commitment from both parties involved.
   2. Boundaries in Reconciliation: Set and respect boundaries while rebuilding trust.

IV. Abusive Relationships: Recognizing Signs and Seeking Help When Necessary

A. Identifying Signs of Abuse

   1. Physical Abuse: Recognize signs of physical harm or aggression in relationships.
   2. Emotional Abuse: Understand the signs of emotional abuse, such as manipulation and control.
   3. Isolation: Be aware of attempts to isolate you from friends and family.

B. Seeking Help

   1. Trusted Confidant: Talk to a trusted friend, family member, or counsellor about your concerns.

2. Hotlines and Support Services: Access hotlines and support services for individuals in abusive relationships.
3. Legal Resources: Learn about legal resources available for those seeking protection from abusive partners.

Building and maintaining healthy relationships is a fundamental aspect of personal development for teenagers. By acquiring conflict resolution skills, setting healthy boundaries, understanding the power of forgiveness, and recognizing the signs of abusive relationships, teenagers can create and maintain positive, respectful, and safe connections with others. Remember that seeking help and support when necessary is a sign of strength, and every individual deserves to be in relationships that promote their well-being and happiness.

CHAPTER 13: Bridging the Generation Gap

Navigating the generation gap can be challenging, but effective communication and understanding can bridge the divide. In this chapter, we'll explore effective parent-teen communication, tips for connecting with parents, and share real conversations with teens.

Effective Parent-Teen Communication

Breaking Down Barriers

Effective communication with parents is essential for healthy family dynamics. We'll discuss:

- Active Listening: How to truly hear and understand your parents' perspectives.
- Expressing Yourself: Strategies for sharing your thoughts, feelings, and concerns with your parents.
- Respecting Differences: The importance of respecting generational differences and values.
- Conflict Resolution: Techniques for resolving conflicts with parents constructively.

Effective Communication with Parents: Active Listening, Expressing Yourself, Respecting Differences, and Conflict Resolution - Advice for Teenagers

Navigating relationships with parents during the teenage years can be challenging, as both parents and teenagers undergo significant changes. Effective communication plays a pivotal role in building positive relationships with parents. This guide offers advice to teenagers on key aspects of communication with their parents, including active listening, expressing themselves, respecting generational differences, and resolving conflicts constructively. By mastering these skills, teenagers can foster understanding, empathy, and healthy communication in their relationships with their parents.

I. Active Listening: How to Truly Hear and Understand Your Parents' Perspectives

A. The Value of Active Listening
   1. Mutual Understanding: Recognize that active listening fosters mutual understanding and respect.
   2. Deeper Connection: Understand that active listening strengthens your connection with your parents.

B. Techniques for Active Listening

   1. Maintain Eye Contact: Show attentiveness by maintaining eye contact during conversations.
   2. Avoid Interruptions: Practice patience by refraining from interrupting while your parents speak.
   3. Reflect and Clarify: Reflect on what you've heard and seek clarification when necessary.
   4. Empathize: Put yourself in your parents' shoes to understand their perspectives better.

II. Expressing Yourself: Strategies for Sharing Your Thoughts, Feelings, and Concerns with Your Parents

A. The Importance of Self-Expression

   1. Building Trust: Understand that self-expression builds trust and strengthens relationships.
   2. Emotional Well-Being: Recognize that expressing your feelings is vital for your emotional well-being.

B. Strategies for Effective Self-Expression

   1. Choose the Right Time: Select an appropriate time to have open and honest conversations with your parents.
   2. Use "I" Statements: Frame your thoughts and feelings using "I" statements to express yourself without blame.
   3. Be Specific: Provide specific examples or situations to help your parents understand your perspective.

4. Stay Calm: Keep your emotions in check and maintain a calm demeanour during discussions.

III. Respecting Differences: The Importance of Respecting Generational Differences and Values

A. Acknowledging Generational Differences

   1. Different Perspectives: Understand that your parents' upbringing and experiences may lead to different viewpoints.
   2. Respect for Experience: Recognize the wisdom that comes from your parents' life experiences.

B. Strategies for Respecting Differences

   1. Open-Mindedness: Approach conversations with an open mind and a willingness to learn from your parents.
   2. Seek Common Ground: Identify shared values and beliefs as a basis for understanding.
   3. Patient Dialogue: Engage in patient and respectful dialogue to bridge generational gaps.

IV. Conflict Resolution: Techniques for Resolving Conflicts with Parents Constructively

A. Acknowledging Conflict

   1. Normalizing Conflict: Understand that disagreements are a natural part of parent-teen relationships.

2. Constructive vs. Destructive Conflict: Differentiate between conflicts that lead to growth and those that harm relationships.

B. Techniques for Constructive Conflict Resolution

1. Active Listening (Recall from Section I): Apply active listening techniques to understand your parents' perspective.
2. Stay Calm and Respectful (Recall from Section II): Maintain composure and respect during disagreements.
3. Compromise: Be willing to find common ground and compromise when necessary.
4. Seek Third-Party Help: If conflicts persist, consider involving a neutral third party, such as a family counsellor or therapist.

Effective communication is the cornerstone of building and maintaining positive relationships with parents during the teenage years. By practicing active listening, expressing themselves honestly, respecting generational differences, and resolving conflicts constructively, teenagers can enhance their connections with their parents. Remember that strong parent-teen relationships are built on mutual understanding, empathy, and a willingness to communicate openly. Developing these communication skills will not only benefit teenagers but also contribute to the harmony and well-being of the entire family.

Connecting with Parents

Building Stronger Bonds

Strengthening your connection with your parents is a rewarding endeavour. We'll explore:

- Quality Time: The significance of spending quality time together and creating lasting memories.
- Shared Interests: How finding common interests can strengthen your relationship.
- Empathy and Understanding: The power of empathy in understanding your parents' perspectives.
- Support and Trust: Nurturing trust and support within the parent-teen relationship.

Part IV

Personal Growth

In this section, we'll delve into personal growth topics that are crucial for your development as a teenager. We'll explore empathy, creative thinking, decision-making, problem-solving, and self-awareness.

Chapter 14: Personal Growth/ Developing Empathy

The Power of Understanding Others

Empathy is a cornerstone of meaningful human connections. In this chapter, we'll explore the significance of empathy, its practical application in everyday life.

The Power of Empathy

Connecting Through Understanding

Empathy is the ability to understand and share the feelings of others. We'll discuss:

- Empathy Defined: What empathy is and why it's essential for building strong relationships.
- Empathetic Listening: Techniques for actively listening to others' experiences and emotions.
- Cultivating Empathy: How to develop and nurture your empathetic abilities.
- Empathy in Conflict Resolution: How empathy can facilitate conflict resolution and understanding.

Strengthening the Parent-Teen Relationship: Quality Time, Shared Interests, Empathy, Support, and Trust

Building a strong and positive relationship between teenagers and their parents is essential for both emotional well-being and family harmony. In this guide, we will explore key aspects of nurturing a healthy parent-teen relationship, including the significance of spending quality time together, discovering shared interests, practicing empathy and understanding, and nurturing trust and support. By focusing on these aspects, teenagers can strengthen their bond with their parents and create lasting, meaningful connections.

I. Quality Time: The Significance of Spending Quality Time Together and Creating Lasting Memories

A. The Value of Quality Time
   1. Bonding: Understand that quality time fosters a deeper emotional bond between teenagers and their parents.
   2. Communication: Recognize that spending time together creates opportunities for open and meaningful communication.
B. Strategies for Quality Time
   1. Family Activities: Plan and participate in family activities or outings that everyone enjoys.
   2. Dedicated Time: Set aside dedicated time for one-on-one interactions with each parent.
   3. Device-Free Time: Create device-free zones or hours to enhance in-person interactions.

OWL STRETCHING AND OTHER ISSUES...

4. Shared Interests (Recall from Section II): Engage in activities that align with shared interests to strengthen your connection.

II. Shared Interests: How Finding Common Interests Can Strengthen Your Relationship

A. Identifying Shared Interests
   1. Exploration: Explore and identify activities, hobbies, or interests that both teenagers and parents can enjoy together.
   2. Communication: Have open conversations to discover each other's passions and preferences.
B. Benefits of Shared Interests
   1. Connection: Shared interests create common ground for bonding and connection.
   2. Quality Time (Recall from Section I): Pursuing shared interests enhances the quality of time spent together.
   3. Mutual Learning: Both teenagers and parents can learn from each other when exploring shared interests.

III. Empathy and Understanding: The Power of Empathy in Understanding Your Parents' Perspectives

A. Developing Empathy

   1. Definition: Understand empathy as the ability to understand and share the feelings of another.
   2. Parent's Perspective: Put yourself in your parent's shoes to understand their experiences and challenges.

B. Benefits of Empathy

   1. Conflict Resolution (Recall from Section IV): Empathy aids in resolving conflicts constructively by promoting understanding.
   2. Effective Communication: Empathy enhances communication by allowing both parties to feel heard and validated.

IV. Support and Trust: Nurturing Trust and Support Within the Parent-Teen Relationship

A. Building Trust

   1. Consistency: Recognize the importance of consistency and reliability in building trust.
   2. Transparency: Communicate openly and honestly with your parents to establish trust.

B. Providing Support
   1. Emotional Support: Seek emotional support from your parents when needed, and offer it in return.
   2. Respectful Communication (Recall from Section III): Practice respectful communication to ensure your parents feel supported.
C. Trust and Independence
   1. Balancing Independence: Understand that trust and independence can coexist in a healthy parent-teen relationship.
   2. Responsibility: Take on responsibilities to demonstrate trustworthiness and maturity.

Nurturing a strong parent-teen relationship involves a combination of spending quality time together, discovering shared interests, practicing empathy and understanding, and nurturing trust and support. By focusing on these aspects, teenagers can build and maintain meaningful connections with their parents that contribute to emotional well-being and family harmony. Remember that strong parent-teen relationships are built on mutual respect, open communication, and a willingness to invest time and effort in nurturing the bond.

Empathy in Action

Making a Difference Through Empathy

Empathy has the power to drive positive change in the world. We'll explore:

- Empathy for Social Change: How empathy can be a catalyst for social justice and advocacy.
- Empathy in Leadership: The role of empathy in effective leadership and teamwork.
- Empathy in Relationships: The impact of empathy on personal relationships and connections.
- Teens Making a Difference: Inspiring stories of teenagers who have used their empathetic abilities to make a positive impact on their communities.

Examples illustrating the importance and impact of empathy in various aspects of teenagers' lives:

1. Empathy for Social Change:
    A. Volunteerism: A teenager volunteers at a local soup kitchen, where they empathize with the struggles of individuals experiencing homelessness. This empathy drives them to initiate a campaign to raise awareness about homelessness issues in their community.

- B. Climate Activism: A teenager deeply empathizes with the devastating effects of climate change on vulnerable communities around the world. They become a passionate advocate for climate action, organizing school strikes and community clean-up events.

2. Empathy in Leadership:

    A. School Club President: A teenager leads a school club focused on mental health awareness. Through active listening and empathy, they create a safe space for students to share their struggles and seek help when needed.

    B. Team Captain: As the captain of their soccer team, a teenager understands the diverse strengths and challenges of each team member. They use empathy to motivate and support teammates, fostering a cohesive and successful team environment.

3. Empathy in Relationships:

    A. Conflict Resolution: Two friends have a disagreement. Instead of escalating the conflict, one teenager empathizes with their friend's perspective, leading to a constructive conversation and a resolution that strengthens their friendship.

    B. Supportive Sibling: A teenager shows empathy towards their younger sibling, who is struggling with schoolwork. They offer help without judgment, creating a trusting sibling relationship built on mutual understanding.

4. Teens Making a Difference:

    A. Youth Mentor: A teenager with a background in art mentors underprivileged youth in their neighbourhood. Through patience and empathy, they help these children express themselves and develop confidence in their abilities.

    B. Anti-Bullying Advocate: A teenager who experienced bullying firsthand becomes an advocate against bullying in their school. They use their empathy to support victims, raise awareness, and promote a culture of kindness.

These examples demonstrate how empathy can be a powerful force for positive change in the lives of teenagers and the communities they are a part of. Empathy fosters understanding, drives action, and enhances relationships, ultimately contributing to a more compassionate and just society.

Chapter 15: Fostering Creative Thinking

Unleashing Your Creative Potential

Creativity is a valuable skill that can drive innovation and personal growth. In this chapter, we'll explore strategies for cultivating creativity.

Cultivating Creativity

Unlocking Your Creative Mind

Creativity is not limited to the arts; it encompasses problem-solving and innovative thinking in all areas of life. We'll discuss:

- The Creative Process: How creativity works and how to tap into your creative potential.
- Overcoming Creative Blocks: Techniques for overcoming obstacles that hinder creative thinking.
- Creative Exercises: Activities to spark your imagination and boost creative thinking.
- Creative Collaboration: The power of collaboration in generating innovative ideas.

Unleashing Your Creative Potential: A Guide for Teenagers

Creativity is a powerful and essential skill that can enhance various aspects of a teenager's life, from academic success to personal growth. In this guide, we will explore the creative process, overcoming creative blocks, engaging in creative exercises, and the benefits of creative collaboration. By embracing creativity, teenagers can unlock their creative potential, cultivate innovation, and approach challenges with fresh perspectives.

I. The Creative Process: How Creativity Works and How to Tap into Your Creative Potential

A. Understanding the Creative Process
   1. Inspiration: Recognize that creativity often begins with inspiration, whether from experiences, observations, or curiosity.
   2. Incubation: Understand that creative ideas may need time to incubate in your mind, allowing connections to form.
   3. Illumination: Embrace the "Aha!" moments when ideas suddenly come to you, often unexpectedly.
   4. Verification: Realize that verifying and refining your creative ideas is a critical step in the process.

B. Techniques to Tap into Your Creative Potential

   1. Mindfulness: Practice mindfulness to heighten your awareness of the world around you, sparking new ideas.
   2. Diverse Experiences: Seek out diverse experiences, such as reading, travel, or trying new activities, to fuel your creativity.
   3. Questioning: Challenge assumptions and ask "What if?" questions to stimulate creative thinking.
   4. Playfulness: Embrace playfulness and experimentation as essential elements of creativity.

II. Overcoming Creative Blocks: Techniques for Overcoming Obstacles that Hinder Creative Thinking

A. Identifying Creative Blocks

   1. Fear of Failure: Recognize that fear of failure can stifle creativity by causing self-doubt.
   2. Perfectionism: Understand that perfectionism can hinder progress by setting unrealistically high standards.
   3. Overthinking: Realize that overanalysing can paralyze creative thinking.

B. Techniques to Overcome Creative Blocks

   1. Embrace Failure: Shift your perspective on failure, viewing it as a valuable learning opportunity.

2. Set Realistic Goals: Adjust your expectations and set achievable goals to combat perfectionism.
3. Mindfulness and Relaxation: Practice relaxation techniques to calm your mind and reduce overthinking.
4. Collaboration (Recall from Section IV): Collaborate with others to gain fresh perspectives and creative solutions.

III. Creative Exercises: Activities to Spark Your Imagination and Boost Creative Thinking

A. Creative Writing Prompts
   1. Journaling: Engage in daily journaling to explore your thoughts and feelings, fostering self-expression and creativity.
   2. Storytelling: Create short stories or poems inspired by writing prompts to develop narrative skills.

B. Visual Arts
   1. Sketching: Dedicate time to sketching or doodling, allowing your creativity to flow through visual art.
   2. Collage: Make collages using magazines, newspapers, or found objects to explore composition and symbolism.

C. Music and Sound

   1. Songwriting: Experiment with songwriting to express emotions and stories through music.
   2. Soundscapes: Create soundscapes by recording and editing environmental sounds to convey atmospheres or emotions.

D. Problem-Solving

   1. Brainstorming: Practice brainstorming sessions with friends to generate a wide range of ideas for projects or challenges.
   2. Reverse Thinking: Challenge yourself by brainstorming solutions in reverse order, starting with the end goal.

IV. Creative Collaboration: The Power of Collaboration in Generating Innovative Ideas

A. The Benefits of Collaborative Creativity

   1. Diverse Perspectives: Collaborating with others brings diverse perspectives and ideas to the table.
   2. Cross-Pollination: Different backgrounds and experiences lead to cross-pollination of ideas, resulting in innovation.

B. Techniques for Effective Creative Collaboration

   1. Active Listening (Recall from Section III): Actively listen to your collaborators to understand their viewpoints.
   2. Feedback: Provide constructive feedback and accept feedback graciously to refine ideas collectively.
   3. Roles and Responsibilities: Clarify roles and responsibilities within the collaboration to ensure efficient progress.

Conclusion

Creativity is a valuable asset that teenagers can develop and nurture throughout their lives. By understanding the creative process, overcoming creative blocks, engaging in creative exercises, and embracing creative collaboration, teenagers can harness their creative potential and apply it to various aspects of their lives, from problem-solving to personal expression. Cultivating creativity not only sparks innovation but also fosters a sense of fulfilment and self-discovery, making it an essential skill for personal and professional growth.

Innovative Ideas from Teens

Youthful Ingenuity

Teenagers are known for their innovative ideas and fresh perspectives. We'll explore:

- Tech and Innovation: Teen-led innovations in technology, science, and engineering.
- Art and Expression: Creative endeavours in the arts, including music, visual arts, and literature.
- Social Impact: How some teens have used their creativity to address social and environmental challenges.
- Entrepreneurial Ventures: Inspiring stories of young entrepreneurs who turned their creative ideas into successful businesses.

Tech and Innovation: Teen-led Innovations in Technology, Science, and Engineering

1. Gitanjali Rao - At just 15, Gitanjali Rao was named TIME magazine's first-ever Kid of the Year in 2020 for her innovative work. She developed a device to detect lead in water, addressing a critical issue in water safety.
2. Rishab Jain - Rishab, a teenage innovator, created an AI-driven tool to improve the targeting of cancer cells during radiation therapy. His innovation has the potential to enhance cancer treatment effectiveness.

Art and Expression: Creative Endeavours in the Arts

1. Grace VanderWaal - Grace won America's Got Talent at the age of 12 with her unique singing and

songwriting talent. She continues to inspire through her music and has released several successful albums.
2. Tyler Gordon - Tyler is a young visual artist known for his breathtaking portraits of influential figures. He has used his art to raise awareness about social issues and inspire change.

Social Impact: How Some Teens Have Used Their Creativity to Address Social and Environmental Challenges

1. Xiye Bastida - Xiye is a climate activist and co-founder of the Re-Earth Initiative. She uses her creative skills in public speaking, storytelling, and advocacy to raise awareness about climate change and inspire action.
2. Haile Thomas - Haile founded the Happy Organization, which focuses on empowering young people to make healthier food choices. Through cooking, education, and community engagement, she addresses issues related to nutrition and food justice.

Entrepreneurial Ventures: Inspiring Stories of Young Entrepreneurs

1. Mikaila Ulmer - Mikaila started her business, Me & the Bees Lemonade, at the age of 4. She uses her

creativity to craft unique lemonade recipes while advocating for bee conservation.
2. Shubham Banerjee - Shubham created a low-cost Braille printer using LEGO Mindstorms. His innovative spirit led to the founding of Braigo Labs, a company dedicated to developing affordable technology for the visually impaired.

These examples highlight how teenagers can channel their creativity into making a positive impact in various fields, from technology and the arts to social and environmental causes. These young innovators and artists serve as inspirational role models for their peers, demonstrating the immense potential of creative thinking and action at a young age.

These examples demonstrate that creativity knows no bounds, and teenagers have the potential to drive meaningful change through their innovative thinking.

Chapter 16: Decision Making and Problem Solving

Navigating Life's Challenges

Effective decision-making and problem-solving skills are essential for success in various aspects of life. In this chapter, we'll explore strategies for making informed decisions, approaches to problem-solving, and share real-life decision-making stories.

Making Informed Decisions

Empowering Yourself with Knowledge

Informed decision-making is crucial for making choices that align with your goals and values. We'll discuss:

- Gathering Information: How to research and gather the facts needed to make informed decisions.
- Assessing Risks and Benefits: Evaluating the potential outcomes and consequences of your choices.
- Balancing Emotion and Logic: The importance of both emotional intelligence and logical reasoning in decision-making.
- Seeking Guidance: When and how to seek advice from trusted mentors, family members, or professionals.

Empowering Teenagers in Decision-Making: Gathering Information, Assessing Risks and Benefits, Balancing Emotion and Logic, and Seeking Guidance

The ability to make informed decisions is a crucial skill that teenagers can develop to navigate the challenges of adolescence and beyond. In this guide, we will explore key aspects of effective decision-making, including gathering information, assessing risks and benefits, balancing emotion and logic, and seeking guidance. By mastering these skills, teenagers can approach decision-making with confidence, ensuring their choices align with their goals and values.

I. Gathering Information: How to Research and Gather the Facts Needed to Make Informed Decisions

A. The Value of Gathering Information
   1. Informed Choices: Recognize that gathering information enables you to make well-informed choices.
   2. Minimizing Regrets: Understand that thorough research reduces the likelihood of regrets or unforeseen consequences.

B. Strategies for Gathering Information
   1. Online Research: Utilize reputable websites, articles, and databases to gather information related to your decision.

2. Interviews: Seek advice and insights from experts, professionals, or individuals with relevant experience.
3. Reading Books and Literature: Explore books, journals, or literature that provide valuable perspectives on your decision.
4. Peer Discussions: Engage in discussions with peers who may have faced similar decisions.

II. Assessing Risks and Benefits: Evaluating the Potential Outcomes and Consequences of Your Choices

A. Identifying Risks and Benefits

1. List Outcomes: Create a list of potential outcomes, both positive and negative, associated with your decision.
2. Probability Assessment: Estimate the likelihood of each outcome occurring.

B. Weighing Risks and Benefits

1. Impact Assessment: Evaluate the significance and consequences of each outcome.
2. Prioritization: Prioritize outcomes based on their importance to your goals and values.

III. Balancing Emotion and Logic: The Importance of Both Emotional Intelligence and Logical Reasoning in Decision-Making

A. Acknowledging Emotions

   1. Recognize Emotions: Identify and acknowledge your emotions related to the decision.
   2. Emotional Awareness: Practice emotional intelligence by understanding the source and nature of your feelings.

B. Applying Logical Reasoning

   1. Critical Thinking: Employ critical thinking skills to analyse information objectively.
   2. Pros and Cons: Create a pros and cons list to structure your logical analysis.

C. Finding Balance

   1. Integration: Integrate both emotional and logical aspects into your decision-making process.
   2. Reflection: Take time to reflect on how your emotions and logic align with your values and goals.

IV. Seeking Guidance: When and How to Seek Advice from Trusted Mentors, Family Members, or Professionals

A. Recognizing the Need for Guidance

   1. Complex Decisions: Understand that seeking guidance is beneficial for complex or impactful decisions.

2. Lack of Expertise: Seek advice when you lack expertise or experience in a particular area.
B. Whom to Seek Guidance From
   1. Trusted Mentors: Turn to mentors, teachers, or older individuals you respect and trust.
   2. Family Members: Engage in open discussions with family members who have your best interests at heart.
   3. Professionals: Consult professionals or experts in relevant fields for specialized advice.
C. Effective Communication
   1. Clear Questions: Prepare clear and specific questions to ensure you receive the guidance you need.
   2. Active Listening (Recall from Section III): Actively listen to the advice provided and consider it in your decision-making process.

Empowering teenagers in decision-making involves mastering the skills of gathering information, assessing risks and benefits, balancing emotion and logic, and seeking guidance when necessary. By honing these abilities, teenagers can approach decisions with confidence and ensure that their choices align with their values and goals. Effective decision-making not only helps teenagers navigate the complexities of adolescence but also sets the foundation for making sound choices in adulthood.

Approaches to Problem Solving

Effective Strategies for Tackling Challenges

Problem-solving is a valuable skill that allows you to overcome obstacles and find solutions to complex issues. We'll explore:

- Defining the Problem: How to identify and clarify the specific challenge you're facing.
- Generating Solutions: Techniques for brainstorming and developing potential solutions.
- Evaluating Options: Assessing the pros and cons of each solution and selecting the best course of action.
- Implementing and Adjusting: Taking action, monitoring progress, and making adjustments as needed.

Teenagers' Guide to Effective Problem-Solving: Defining, Generating, Evaluating, Implementing, and Adjusting

Effective problem-solving is a valuable skill that empowers teenagers to overcome challenges and make informed decisions. In this guide, we will explore the essential steps of problem-solving: defining the problem, generating solutions, evaluating options, implementing and adjusting. By mastering these steps, teenagers can approach problems with confidence, develop creative solutions, and achieve their goals.

I. Defining the Problem: Identifying and Clarifying the Specific Challenge You're Facing

A. Recognizing the Importance of Problem Definition
    1. Clarity: Understand that defining the problem clearly is the foundation of effective problem-solving.
    2. Focus: Realize that a well-defined problem helps you stay focused on the issue at hand.
B. Strategies for Defining the Problem
    1. Ask Questions: Use open-ended questions to explore the nature and scope of the problem.
    2. Collect Data: Gather relevant information and data to gain a comprehensive understanding.
    3. Break It Down: Divide complex problems into smaller, manageable components for analysis.

II. Generating Solutions: Techniques for Brainstorming and Developing Potential Solutions

A. Embracing Creativity in Solution Generation
    1. Divergent Thinking: Understand that brainstorming involves exploring a wide range of ideas without judgment.
    2. Unconventional Ideas: Encourage thinking outside the box to consider unconventional solutions.

B. Strategies for Generating Solutions

   1. Brainstorming Sessions: Organize brainstorming sessions with peers or mentors to gather diverse ideas.
   2. Mind Mapping: Create visual mind maps to connect and expand on ideas.
   3. Reverse Engineering: Consider the desired outcome and work backward to explore possible solutions.

II. Evaluating Options: Assessing the Pros and Cons of Each Solution and Selecting the Best Course of Action

A. The Importance of Evaluation

   1. Informed Decisions: Recognize that evaluating options allows you to make informed choices.
   2. Risk Management: Understand that assessing pros and cons helps you anticipate potential challenges.

B. Strategies for Evaluating Options

   1. Pros and Cons Lists: Create lists to systematically compare the advantages and disadvantages of each solution.
   2. Criteria-Based Evaluation: Establish criteria (e.g., feasibility, impact) to assess solutions objectively.

3. Seeking Input: Consult trusted individuals for their insights and perspectives on the options.

IV. Implementing and Adjusting: Taking Action, Monitoring Progress, and Making Adjustments as Needed

A. Taking Action
   1. Commitment: Understand that taking action requires dedication and follow-through.
   2. Small Steps: Break down the implementation into manageable steps to avoid feeling overwhelmed.
B. Monitoring Progress
   1. Tracking: Use journals or progress trackers to monitor the implementation process.
   2. Feedback (Recall from Section II): Seek feedback from others to gauge the effectiveness of your chosen solution.
C. Making Adjustments
   1. Flexibility: Be open to adapting your approach if you encounter unexpected challenges or changes in circumstances.
   2. Continuous Improvement: Embrace a growth mindset and view setbacks as opportunities for improvement.

Effective problem-solving is a skill that empowers teenagers to face challenges with confidence and creativity. By following the steps of problem-solving, including defining the problem, generating solutions, evaluating options, and implementing and adjusting, teenagers can tackle a wide range of issues, from academic challenges to personal goals. Cultivating these problem-solving skills not only enhances decision-making but also equips teenagers with a valuable tool for success in their academic, personal, and professional lives.

Chapter 17: Embracing Self-Awareness

The Path to Self-Discovery

Self-awareness is the foundation of personal growth and a key to leading a fulfilling life. In this chapter, we'll explore the journey to self-discovery, provide self-awareness tools, and share personal transformations.

The Journey to Self-Discovery

Getting to Know Yourself

The journey of self-awareness involves introspection, reflection, and self-acceptance. We'll discuss:

- Self-Reflection: The importance of introspection and understanding your thoughts and feelings.
- Identifying Strengths and Weaknesses: Recognizing your unique talents and areas for growth.
- Values and Beliefs: Exploring your core values and beliefs and how they influence your choices.
- Emotional Intelligence: Understanding and managing your emotions effectively.

Self-Awareness Tools

Practical Strategies for Self-Discovery

Self-awareness can be cultivated through various tools and practices. We'll explore:

- Journaling: How keeping a journal can facilitate self-reflection and personal growth.
- Mindfulness and Meditation: Techniques for cultivating mindfulness and self-awareness.
- Personality Assessments: The benefits of personality assessments in understanding your traits and tendencies.
- Feedback and Self-Assessment: The value of seeking feedback from others and self-assessing your progress.

Teenagers' Guide to Self-Discovery and Personal Growth: Journaling, Mindfulness, Personality Assessments, Feedback, and Self-Assessment

Self-discovery and personal growth are vital aspects of a teenager's journey toward becoming a well-rounded and self-aware individual. In this guide, we will explore various techniques that can aid teenagers in their pursuit of self-improvement and personal growth, including journaling, mindfulness and meditation, personality assessments, and the importance of feedback and self-assessment.

I. Journaling: How Keeping a Journal Can Facilitate Self-Reflection and Personal Growth

A. Recognizing the Power of Journaling

   1. Self-Reflection: Understand that journaling is a tool for self-reflection, helping you better understand your thoughts, emotions, and experiences.
   2. Problem Solving: Realize that journaling can serve as a problem-solving tool, allowing you to explore challenges and brainstorm solutions.

B. Strategies for Effective Journaling

   1. Consistency: Make journaling a regular habit, whether daily or weekly, to foster self-awareness.
   2. Openness: Be open and honest in your writing, as it is a private space for self-expression.
   3. Goals and Intentions: Set specific goals for your journaling practice, such as tracking personal growth or exploring your emotions.

II. Mindfulness and Meditation: Techniques for Cultivating Mindfulness and Self-Awareness

A. Embracing Mindfulness

   1. Present Moment Awareness: Understand that mindfulness involves being fully present in the current moment, free from judgment.

2. Stress Reduction: Recognize that mindfulness can reduce stress and enhance overall well-being.

B. Mindfulness and Meditation Practices

   1. Breath Awareness: Practice focusing on your breath to anchor yourself in the present moment.
   2. Body Scan: Perform body scan meditations to connect with physical sensations and release tension.
   3. Guided Meditations: Utilize guided meditations, available through apps or online resources, to explore mindfulness.

III. Personality Assessments: The Benefits of Personality Assessments in Understanding Your Traits and Tendencies

A. Exploring Personality Assessments

   1. Self-Awareness: Understand that personality assessments can offer valuable insights into your unique traits, strengths, and weaknesses.
   2. Interpersonal Relationships: Realize that understanding your personality can improve communication and relationships with others.

B. Popular Personality Assessments

   1. Myers-Briggs Type Indicator (MBTI): Explore your personality type through the MBTI to gain insights into your preferences and tendencies.

2. Big Five Personality Traits: Assess your openness, conscientiousness, extraversion, agreeableness, and neuroticism to understand your core traits.

IV. Feedback and Self-Assessment: The Value of Seeking Feedback from Others and Self-Assessing Your Progress

A. Embracing Feedback
   1. Continuous Improvement: Recognize that feedback is a catalyst for personal growth, helping you identify areas for improvement.
   2. Diverse Perspectives: Understand that feedback from others provides different viewpoints that enhance self-awareness.
B. Self-Assessment
   1. Goal Review: Regularly assess your progress toward personal goals and objectives.
   2. Strengths and Weaknesses: Reflect on your strengths and weaknesses to identify areas where you can enhance your skills.

Self-discovery and personal growth are lifelong journeys that teenagers can actively engage in. By incorporating techniques such as journaling, mindfulness and meditation, personality assessments, and seeking feedback and self-assessment into their lives, teenagers can foster self-awareness, enhance their personal development, and make informed choices that align with their values and aspirations. These practices empower teenagers to become resilient, adaptable, and self-aware individuals prepared for the challenges and opportunities that lie ahead.

CHAPTER 18: Personal Hygiene

The Importance of Teenage Hygiene and Seeking Help When Needed

Maintaining good hygiene is an essential aspect of a teenager's overall health and well-being. Proper hygiene not only helps you feel confident and comfortable but also plays a vital role in preventing illness and promoting self-esteem. In this chapter, we'll explore the importance of teenage hygiene, offer practical hygiene tips, and discuss where to turn when faced with hygiene-related problems.

The Significance of Teenage Hygiene

Good hygiene habits are crucial for teenagers as they go through physical and emotional changes.

Here's why maintaining proper hygiene matters:

1. Health and Well-being: Good hygiene practices help prevent the spread of illness and reduce the risk of infections.
2. Self-Esteem: Feeling clean and fresh enhances self-esteem and confidence.
3. Social Acceptance: Good hygiene is essential for positive social interactions and building healthy relationships with peers.

OWL STRETCHING AND OTHER ISSUES...

4. Personal Comfort: Proper hygiene ensures comfort and reduces discomfort caused by body odor, acne, or other hygiene-related issues.
5. Puberty and Hormones: Teenagers experience hormonal changes that can affect their skin, hair, and body odor. Maintaining good hygiene can mitigate the impact of these changes.

Practical Teenage Hygiene Tips

1. Daily Shower or Bath: Aim to shower or bathe daily to cleanse your body and remove sweat, dirt, and bacteria.
2. Oral Hygiene: Brush your teeth at least twice a day and floss once daily to maintain good oral health and prevent dental issues.
3. Hair Care: Wash your hair as needed, depending on your hair type and activity level. Use shampoo and conditioner appropriate for your hair.
4. Deodorant: Apply deodorant or antiperspirant to control body odor. Consider consulting a dermatologist for recommendations if you experience excessive sweating.
5. Face Care: Develop a skincare routine that includes washing your face with a gentle cleanser and using sunscreen to protect your skin from sun damage.

6. Hand Washing: Wash your hands regularly, especially before eating or after using the restroom, to prevent the spread of germs.
7. Clothing and Laundry: Change into clean clothes daily and launder them regularly. Pay attention to undergarments and socks to prevent odour.
8. Menstrual Hygiene: If you menstruate, practice proper menstrual hygiene using sanitary products like pads or tampons. Change them regularly.
9. Nail and Foot Care: Trim your nails and keep them clean. Pay attention to foot hygiene, especially if you play sports or are physically active.

Where to Go When There Is a Problem

Despite your best efforts, you may encounter hygiene-related issues at times. It's essential to know where to turn for help and guidance:

1. Family and Trusted Adults: Talk to your parents, guardians, or another trusted adult about hygiene concerns. They can offer guidance and support.
2. School Nurse: If you experience hygiene-related problems at school, don't hesitate to seek assistance from the school nurse. They can provide advice and resources.
3. Medical Professionals: For skin issues, excessive sweating, or other persistent hygiene problems,

consult a dermatologist or healthcare provider. They can diagnose and treat underlying conditions.
4. Dental Check-ups: Visit your dentist regularly for check-ups and dental hygiene advice.
5. Mental Health Professionals: Sometimes, hygiene problems can be related to mental health issues like depression or anxiety. Seek help from a therapist or counsellor if needed.
6. Peer Support: Share concerns with close friends who can offer support and understanding.

Conclusion

Teenage hygiene is a critical aspect of overall health and well-being. By maintaining good hygiene practices and seeking help when needed, teenagers can navigate the physical and emotional changes of adolescence with confidence and comfort. Remember that maintaining hygiene is a lifelong skill that contributes to a healthy, happy, and fulfilling life.

Basic Skills

Cooking

Cooking is a valuable life skill that can be fun and rewarding. Here are some tips and advice for teenagers who want to learn how to cook:

Start with the Basics:

Begin with simple recipes and gradually work your way up to more complex dishes. Mastering basic cooking techniques like chopping, sautéing, and boiling is essential.

Gather the Right Tools:

Invest in basic kitchen equipment such as pots, pans, knives, cutting boards, measuring cups, and utensils. Having the right tools makes cooking easier and safer.

Learn to Follow Recipes:

Start by following recipes from cookbooks, websites, or cooking apps. Pay close attention to measurements and instructions.

Practice Knife Skills:

Proper knife skills are essential for efficient and safe cooking. Learn how to chop, dice, and mince vegetables and other ingredients.

Safety First:

Always be cautious in the kitchen. Supervision from an adult may be necessary, especially when working with sharp objects, hot surfaces, or appliances.

Experiment and Get Creative:

Don't be afraid to experiment with flavours and ingredients. Cooking allows for creativity, so feel free to add your own twist to recipes.

Plan Your Meals:

Planning meals in advance can help you make healthier choices and save time. Create a weekly menu and a shopping list.

Learn to Cook a Few Signature Dishes:

Discover a few recipes you love and become proficient in making them. Having a few go-to dishes can be impressive and satisfying.

Understand Food Safety:

Learn about food safety practices, such as proper storage, handling, and cooking temperatures to prevent foodborne illnesses.

Clean as You Go:

Cleaning up as you cook will make the process more manageable and ensure you have a tidy kitchen when you're finished.

Don't Be Discouraged by Mistakes:

Everyone makes mistakes in the kitchen. If a dish doesn't turn out as expected, learn from it and try again. Cooking is a skill that improves with practice.

Seek Guidance:

Don't hesitate to ask for help or advice from experienced cooks or family members. They can provide valuable tips and guidance.

Practice Time Management:

Cooking can take time, so learn to manage your time effectively. Start with recipes that fit your schedule, and plan accordingly.

Explore Different Cuisines:

Try cooking dishes from various cuisines around the world. It's a great way to expand your culinary horizons and taste new flavours.

Enjoy the Process:

Cooking should be enjoyable, so have fun while you're in the kitchen. Share your creations with family and friends to spread the joy of cooking.

Remember, cooking is a lifelong skill, and the more you practice, the better you'll become. It's a valuable skill that can lead to healthier eating habits, save you money, and impress your loved ones If you're a first-time cook, it's best to start with simple recipes that don't require a lot of ingredients or advanced cooking techniques. Here are some easy recipes to get you started:

Scrambled Eggs:

Ingredients: Eggs, butter or oil, salt, pepper

Instructions: Whisk eggs in a bowl, add a pinch of salt and pepper. Heat butter or oil in a pan over medium-low heat. Pour in the eggs and stir gently until they're cooked to your liking.

Pasta with Tomato Sauce:

Ingredients: Pasta (e.g., spaghetti), canned tomato sauce, salt, pepper, olive oil, grated Parmesan cheese (optional)

Instructions: Cook pasta according to package instructions. Heat olive oil in a saucepan, add tomato sauce, season with salt and pepper, and simmer for a few minutes. Toss the cooked pasta in the sauce. Top with grated Parmesan cheese if desired.

Grilled Cheese Sandwich:

Ingredients: Bread, butter, cheese slices

Instructions: Butter one side of each bread slice. Place cheese between two slices with the buttered sides facing out. Heat a pan over medium heat and cook the sandwich until both sides are golden brown and the cheese is melted.

Stir-Fry Chicken and Vegetables:

Ingredients: Boneless chicken breast or thigh, vegetables (e.g., bell peppers, broccoli, carrots), soy sauce, garlic, ginger, vegetable oil

Instructions: Cut chicken into bite-sized pieces. Heat oil in a pan, add minced garlic and ginger, then add chicken. Once chicken is cooked, add sliced vegetables and stir-fry until tender. Finish with a splash of soy sauce.

Baked Potatoes:

Ingredients: Potatoes, olive oil, salt, toppings (e.g., sour cream, chives, cheese)

Instructions: Preheat the oven to 400°F (200°C). Scrub and dry the potatoes, then rub them with olive oil and sprinkle with salt. Pierce them with a fork several times. Bake for about an hour until they're tender. Serve with your choice of toppings.

Homemade Quesadillas:

Ingredients: Flour tortillas, cheese, cooked chicken (optional), salsa (optional)

Instructions: Place a tortilla in a hot, dry pan. Sprinkle cheese and add cooked chicken and salsa (if desired) on one half of the tortilla. Fold the other half over and cook until the tortilla is crispy and the cheese is melted. Flip and cook the other side.

Rice and Beans:

Ingredients: Rice, canned beans (e.g., black beans or kidney beans), onion, garlic, cumin, salt, vegetable oil

Instructions: Cook rice according to package instructions. In a separate pan, sauté chopped onion and minced garlic in oil until softened. Add drained and rinsed beans, a pinch of cumin, and salt. Cook until heated through. Serve over rice.

These recipes are beginner-friendly and a great way to start building your cooking skills. As you become more comfortable in the kitchen, you can experiment with more complex dishes and flavours.

Cleaning

Cleaning a house can be a daunting task, especially for teenagers who may not have much experience with household chores. Here are some tips and advice on how to clean a house effectively:

Make a Cleaning Schedule:

Create a cleaning schedule that outlines what needs to be cleaned and when. This will help you stay organized and prevent chores from piling up.

Gather Cleaning Supplies:

Before you start, gather all the necessary cleaning supplies, such as brooms, mops, vacuum cleaners, dust cloths, cleaning solutions, and garbage bags.

Declutter First:

Begin by decluttering each room. Put away items that are out of place and consider donating or throwing away things you no longer need.

Start from the Top:

When cleaning a room, start from the top and work your way down. Dust ceiling fans, light fixtures, and shelves before cleaning surfaces and floors.

Clean Room by Room:

Focus on one room at a time to avoid feeling overwhelmed. Clean each room thoroughly before moving on to the next.

Dust and Wipe Surfaces:

Dust all surfaces, including shelves, tables, and countertops. Use appropriate cleaning solutions for different surfaces (e.g., glass cleaner for mirrors, wood cleaner for wooden surfaces).

Vacuum and Sweep:

Vacuum carpets, rugs, and upholstery. Sweep and mop hard floors. Pay special attention to corners and under furniture.

Clean Kitchen and Bathroom Thoroughly:

These areas tend to require extra attention. Scrub sinks, countertops, and appliances in the kitchen. In the bathroom, clean the toilet, sink, bathtub/shower, and mirrors.

Change Bed Linens:

Don't forget to change bed linens regularly, including sheets, pillowcases, and duvet covers. Launder them according to care instructions.

Empty Trash Bins:

Empty all trash bins in the house and replace the liners as needed. Make sure to take the trash out to the main bin.

Sweep and Tidy Outdoor Areas (if applicable):

If you have outdoor spaces, such as a porch or patio, sweep and tidy them as well.

Don't Forget About Regular Maintenance:

In addition to regular cleaning, remember to perform maintenance tasks like checking smoke detectors, changing air filters, and cleaning out the refrigerator.

Safety First:

Be cautious when using cleaning products, and always follow the instructions on the labels. Ensure proper ventilation while cleaning with chemicals.

Ask for Help if Needed:

If you're unsure about how to clean specific items or areas, don't hesitate to ask for guidance from a trusted adult or use online resources.

Reward Yourself:

After a thorough cleaning session, reward yourself for a job well done. Enjoy a clean and organized living space!

Cleaning a house is a skill that improves with practice. Over time, you'll develop a routine that works for you and makes the task more manageable. Remember that maintaining a clean and organized home can contribute to a healthier and more enjoyable living environment.

Moving into your first flat share:

Moving into university halls or a flat share can be an exciting but challenging experience. Here is some advice to help teenagers navigate this transition successfully:

Communication is Key:

Communication with your roommates or flatmates is essential. Establish open and respectful communication from the beginning. Discuss expectations, boundaries, and any concerns you may have.

Set Ground Rules:

Create a set of basic ground rules for shared spaces, such as the kitchen, bathroom, and common areas. This can help prevent conflicts and maintain a harmonious living environment.

Respect Personal Space:

Be mindful of your roommates' need for privacy and personal space. Knock before entering someone's room and respect their belongings.

Manage Shared Expenses:

Discuss and agree on how shared expenses like rent, utilities, and groceries will be handled. Consider setting up a shared expense tracking system to ensure fairness.

Share Household Chores:

Create a cleaning schedule or chore chart to distribute responsibilities for cleaning common areas. This helps prevent resentment and keeps the living space tidy.

Be Considerate and Tolerant:

Living with others from diverse backgrounds may expose you to different lifestyles and habits. Be open-minded and willing to compromise to accommodate these differences.

Set Study Boundaries:

Establish guidelines for quiet hours or study spaces, especially if you or your roommates have different study habits or schedules.

Respect Noise Levels:

Be mindful of noise, especially during quiet hours. Use headphones when listening to music or watching videos, and keep noise to a minimum when others are studying or resting.

Safety First:

Ensure that your living space is secure. Lock doors and windows when leaving or going to bed, and be cautious about who you allow into your home.

Budget Wisely:

Create a budget to manage your finances effectively. Track your expenses and prioritize essentials like rent, groceries, and utilities.

Handle Conflicts Maturely:

Conflicts can arise in shared living spaces. When they do, address them calmly and constructively. If needed, involve a mediator or residence advisor for help.

Respect Shared Resources:

Be mindful of shared resources like kitchen appliances, toilet paper, and cleaning supplies. Contribute your fair share and replace items when necessary.

Stay Organized:

Keep your personal space tidy and organized to minimize clutter and stress. This will also make it easier to find your belongings.

Stay Safe and Healthy:

Prioritize your health and safety by maintaining good hygiene, following safety guidelines, and looking out for one another.

Get Involved:

Join social or extracurricular activities within your university or flat share community to meet new people and build a support network.

Seek Help When Needed:

If you encounter challenges that you can't resolve on your own, don't hesitate to reach out to university support services, counsellors, or flat share management for assistance.

Moving into university halls or a flat share is an opportunity for personal growth and learning to coexist with others. By being respectful, communicative, and considerate, you can create a positive and enjoyable living experience during your time at university.

Choose life

Choosing a job or university after leaving school is a significant decision that can shape your future. Here are some tips for teenagers on how to make these important choices:

Self-assessment:

Take time to assess your interests, skills, and values. What are you passionate about? What are your strengths and weaknesses? Knowing yourself better will help you make informed decisions.

Explore your interests:

Experiment with different hobbies, extracurricular activities, and volunteer opportunities. This can help you discover what you enjoy and what you might want to pursue in a career or further education.

Set goals:

Define your short-term and long-term goals. What do you want to achieve in the next few years, and where do you see yourself in the future? This can provide a sense of direction.

Research career options:

Explore various careers through online research, informational interviews, and job shadowing. Understanding the requirements and responsibilities of different jobs can help you make an informed choice.

Consider your values:

Think about what is most important to you, such as work-life balance, job stability, salary, and job satisfaction. Make sure your career choice aligns with your values.

Seek advice:

Talk to teachers, counsellors, parents, and professionals in fields you're interested in. They can provide valuable insights and advice.

College or alternative paths:

Decide whether you want to pursue higher education at a university, college, or a vocational school, or if you prefer an alternative path like apprenticeships or online courses.

Explore universities and programs:

Research universities and the programs they offer. Consider factors like location, reputation, cost, and specific programs that align with your interests and career goals.

Financial planning:

Understand the costs of education and how you'll fund it. Look into scholarships, grants, and financial aid options to reduce the burden of student loans.

Internships and part-time jobs:

Gain real-world experience through internships or part-time jobs in your field of interest. This can help you build skills, network, and confirm your career choice.

Visit campuses:

If you're considering higher education, visit the campuses of the universities or colleges you're interested in. This can help you get a feel for the environment and community.

Create a timeline:

Develop a timeline for your decision-making process, application deadlines, and steps to achieve your goals.

Stay adaptable:

Keep in mind that it's okay to change your mind or adjust your plans as you learn and grow. Your career path may evolve over time.

Don't rush:

Avoid making hasty decisions. Take the time you need to make an informed choice that aligns with your interests and goals.

Keep a positive attitude:

Be open to new opportunities and experiences, and remember that it's okay to make mistakes and learn from them. Your career journey is a lifelong process.

Ultimately, choosing a job or university is a personal decision, and there is no one-size-fits-all approach. Take the time to explore your options and make decisions that feel right for you.

Your Teenage Journey, Your Success Story

Your teenage years are a time of growth, self-discovery, and preparation for the future.

By now, you will have acquired a wealth of knowledge, strategies, to help you navigate the complexities of teenage life, develop essential life skills, build meaningful relationships, and embark on a journey of personal growth and self-discovery. Your teenage years are a time of incredible potential, and with the right guidance and mindset, you can truly thrive and create a brighter future for yourself. I wish you all the best for the future and cant wait to see the person you will become.

Milton Keynes UK
Ingram Content Group UK Ltd.
UKHW040212160324
439374UK00004B/206

9 781803 818429